ACT
IN
DOCTRINE

ACT
— IN —
DOCTRINE

Spiritual patterns for turning
from self to the Savior

DAVID A. BEDNAR

DESERET
BOOK

SALT LAKE CITY, UTAH

Library of Congress Cataloging-in-Publication Data
(CIP information on file)
ISBN 978-1-60907-227-8

Printed in the United States of America
Publishers Printing, Salt Lake City, UT

10   9   8   7   6   5   4   3   2   1

To Richard and Lavina Whitney Bednar
and Kay and Nyla Clement Robinson

Contents

ACKNOWLEDGMENTS

I am thankful to my wife, Susan, for her consistent example of Christlike character, her love and loyalty, and her righteous devotion. I also express appreciation to Shauna Swainston for her timely help and support; to Sheri Dew for her enthusiastic encouragement to "press forward" with this book; and to Max Molgard for his insightful and helpful comments about the manuscript.

The publishing team at Deseret Book has worked with professionalism and excellence. Thanks go to Cory Maxwell for his consistently effective work in overseeing the project; Emily Watts for her expert counsel, editing, and assistance in preparing the manuscript for publication; Richard Erickson and Sheryl Dickert Smith for the design; Rachael Ward for the typography; and Laurel Christensen, Elizabeth Alley, and Dallas Petersen for their help with the accompanying DVD and online components of the project. Heartfelt thanks to our family, friends, and associates who have been so instrumental in helping me formulate and refine the ideas presented in this book. I am grateful for all of the individuals, both named and unnamed, who have inspired, supported, and assisted me in writing *Act in Doctrine*.

This book is not an official statement of Church doctrine, policy, or practice, and I alone am responsible for the content of *Act in Doctrine*.

PREFACE

As disciples of the Lord Jesus Christ, our individual responsibility is to learn what we should learn, to live as we know we should live, and to become what the Master would have us become. These three fundamental and interrelated gospel imperatives—learning, acting, and becoming—are central to our spiritual development and happiness in mortality and our progress throughout eternity.

My previous book, *Increase in Learning,* focused upon the doctrines, principles, and patterns related to the learning imperative. *Act in Doctrine* focuses upon the doctrines, principles, and patterns related to our obligation to translate what we know into what we do. And learning and acting in accordance with revealed gospel truth ultimately can invite into our lives the "power to become" (Doctrine and Covenants 11:30) all that the Father's plan of salvation makes possible for us.

One need not have read *Increase in Learning* in order to benefit from *Act in Doctrine.* But the following summary of the basic principles contained in the former book—whether by way of introduction or as a review—may enlarge the reader's understanding.

xi

Increase in Learning: An Overview

Chapter One, "An Individual Responsibility to Learn," stresses the importance of learning in the latter days. We cannot expect the Church as an organization to teach or tell us all of the things we need to know and do to become devoted disciples. The ultimate responsibility for developing spiritual strength and stamina rests upon each and every member of the Church.

Learning by faith and learning from experience are two of the central features of the Father's plan of happiness. The powerful examples of latter-day learners—including Joseph Smith, Brigham Young, Gordon B. Hinckley, and some less well-known members of the Church—highlight for us the importance of continually seeking learning by study and also by faith (see Doctrine and Covenants 88:118).

You and I are here upon the earth to prepare for eternity, to learn how to learn, to learn things that are temporally important and eternally essential, and to assist others in learning wisdom and truth (see Doctrine and Covenants 97:1). Understanding who we are, where we came from, and why we are upon the earth places upon each of us a great responsibility both to learn how to learn and to learn to love learning.

Chapter Two, "Knowledge, Understanding, and Intelligence," explores a hierarchy that exists among the things we can learn. Many facts are helpful or merely interesting to know. Some knowledge is useful to learn and apply. But gospel truths are essential for us to understand and live if we are to become what our Heavenly Father yearns for us to become.

Knowledge refers generally to facts, information, and abilities obtained through experience or education. Using the instrument of our physical bodies and our capacity to reflect and reason, we can gather and analyze facts, organize and interpret information, gain and learn from experience, and identify patterns and relationships. Of the many types of knowledge that can be acquired, spiritual knowledge is the most important, both in mortality and in eternity.

Understanding is the keystone that is erected upon the cornerstone of knowledge and precedes intelligence. Interestingly, the word *understanding* is commonly described in the scriptures in relation to the heart. *Understanding* as used in the scriptures does not refer solely or even primarily to intellectual or cognitive comprehension. Rather, when the Holy Ghost confirms in our hearts as true what we know in our minds, understanding occurs.

Intelligence is the righteous application of knowledge and understanding in action and judgment. It is the capstone constructed upon the cornerstone of knowledge and made stable by the keystone of understanding. You and I may know the right things to do, but intelligence involves more than just knowing. If you and I are intelligent, we will consistently do the right things. Intelligence is living in such a way that the doctrines of the gospel are an active and integral part of who we are, and what we are, and what we do, and what we think.

Appropriately seeking for knowledge, understanding, and intelligence is essential for each of us to become a living member of the Savior's living church (see Doctrine and Covenants 1:30).

Chapter Three, "Prayerful Inquiry: Asking, Seeking, and Knocking," emphasizes patterns of prayerful inquiry that are necessary prerequisites to inspiration and revelation. Three components of prayerful inquiry are emphasized repeatedly in the scriptures: asking, seeking, and knocking. These three interrelated and overlapping elements are vital in the pattern the Lord has employed when giving direction, instruction, and assurance. Honesty, effort, commitment, and persistence are required in asking, seeking, and knocking.

The principle of prayerful inquiry and the pattern of asking, seeking, and knocking suggest three basic responsibilities for each of us as latter-day learners. First, inquiring of the Lord through asking, seeking, and knocking requires and is an expression of faith in the Savior. Second, we should be simultaneously persisting in and remaining patient with this active process. Third, discerning and accepting the will of God in our lives are fundamental elements of prayerful inquiry through asking, seeking, and knocking.

Chapter Four, "Doctrines, Principles, and Applications: A Framework for Gospel Learning," offers a basic and flexible framework for learning about gospel learning. The framework includes three basic elements: doctrines, principles, and applications.

A gospel *doctrine* is a truth of salvation revealed by a loving Heavenly Father. Gospel doctrines are eternal, do not change, and pertain to the eternal progression and exaltation of Heavenly Father's sons and daughters. Doctrines such as the nature of the Godhead, the plan of happiness, and the Atonement of Jesus Christ are foundational, fundamental, and comprehensive.

Gospel doctrines answer the question of "why?" For example, the doctrine of the plan of happiness answers the question of *why* we are here upon the earth. The doctrine of the Atonement explains *why* Jesus is our mediator and advocate with the Father. Basic gospel doctrines are the spiritual foundation for all that we learn, teach, and do—and a vital source of power and strength as we strive to become what the Lord would have us become.

A gospel *principle* is a doctrinally based guideline for the righteous exercise of moral agency. Principles provide direction. Correct principles always are based upon and arise from doctrines, do not change, and answer the question of "what?" Many principles can grow out of and be associated with a single doctrine. For example, the doctrine of the plan of happiness gives rise to such principles as obedience, service, and progression.

A principle is not a behavior or a specific action. Rather, principles provide basic guidelines for behavior and action.

Applications are the actual behaviors, action steps, practices, or procedures by which gospel doctrines and principles are enacted in our lives. Whereas doctrines and principles do not change, applications appropriately can vary according to needs and circumstances. Applications answer the question of "how?"

The framework of doctrines, principles, and applications is a flexible tool that can be used to enhance our gospel learning. It is not a rigid set of definitions or a formula that leads to "correct" answers about which applications and principles are associated with particular gospel doctrines. Rather, it can be a useful aid as we apply the principle of prayerful inquiry and the pattern of asking, seeking, and knocking. If we focus on asking the right questions, we are much more likely to obtain inspired and insightful answers as we work, ponder, search, and pray.

Our tendency as members of the Church is to focus on applications. But as we learn to ask ourselves, "What doctrines and principles, if understood, would help with this challenge?" we come to realize that the answers always are in the doctrines and principles of the gospel.

ACT IN DOCTRINE

The title of this second book comes from a verse in the Doctrine and Covenants: "That every man may *act in doctrine* and principle pertaining to futurity, according to the moral agency which I have given unto him, that every man may be accountable for his own sins in the day of judgment" (Doctrine and Covenants 101:78; emphasis added). This volume builds upon and extends the patterns described in *Increase in Learning* and discusses why we should and how we can "act in doctrine."

We are admonished to search and understand "great knowledge" (2 Nephi 32:7)—even the true knowledge of our Redeemer (see Mosiah 27:36; Helaman 15:13; 3 Nephi 16:4). But we do not learn just to know, and we do not act just to comply or conform. Rather, our learning and acting are to be lastingly transformational as we become new creatures in Christ (see 2 Corinthians 5:17) and offer our whole souls unto God (see Omni 1:26).

Recall that Joseph Smith did not pray simply to know which church was true. He prayed to know which church was true *so he would know which church to join* (see Joseph Smith–History 1:18). And the same truth that led Joseph to the Sacred Grove to "ask in faith" (James 1:6) applies precisely to you and to me. We need to increase in learning of revealed truth so we can act in doctrine and thereby apply what we know and do for righteous purposes.

What we know about the Eternal Father and His plan of happiness, about the Lord Jesus Christ and His Atonement, and about the nature of our relationship to the Father and the Son should influence everything we think, say, and do—and all that we yearn to become. Knowing is an important first step—but it is only a beginning. Because of the gift of moral agency, we are agents blessed with the power and capacity to act and not objects to be acted upon. Thus, what we do with the truths we know and how we "act in doctrine" are essential elements and key indicators of our testimony, conversion, and spiritual development.

As in *Increase in Learning,* I have attempted in this book to relate some of the *spiritual gifts* associated with the companionship of the third member of the Godhead, even the Holy Ghost, to the imperative to act in doctrine. I invite you throughout the book to engage in various learning experiences so you can increasingly "stand independent" (Doctrine and Covenants 78:14) and learn how to find answers to your own questions. Consequently, as you progress through the chapters you will need to read, study, ponder, search, ask, knock, record thoughts and feelings, link, connect, revise, rethink, ask again, start again, and, most important, act. Experiencing this book will require diligent work and sustained commitment. Your willingness to act will invite the Holy Ghost to be your personal teacher of all truth.

Act in Doctrine is formatted with extra-wide margins for recording thoughts, impressions, and questions. Space also is provided at the end of each chapter for (1) recording questions that arise and answers you receive based upon your personal learning, reflecting, and commitments, (2) listing scriptural references related to your learning and acting, and (3) responding to an invitation to learn and act upon the principles discussed in the chapter. This invitation consists of three interrelated questions that should be considered together but responded to individually. Thus, all three questions are repeated at the top of each response page, and the one to be addressed specifically on that page is highlighted.

As you endeavor to act in doctrine, please remember that the truths of the restored gospel of Jesus Christ should be considered in their totality. In other words, attempting to understand a doctrine or principle by relying unduly upon a single scripture or prophetic statement in isolation from all else that has been revealed on the subject generally is misguided. True doctrines and principles are emphasized repeatedly in the standard works, by the prophets and apostles, and through the illuminating and confirming power of the Holy Ghost.

Additional learning resources are available online at seek.deseret book.com. A DVD is also included in the book with a question-and-answer session in which the ideas are explored further in a group setting. Please remember, however, that the written text, the questions to consider, and the additional resources are not complete in and of themselves. Each has been designed to complement and enhance the others.

At the end of each chapter I have suggested related readings that expand on and emphasize the basic concepts taught. Rather than include these readings in the text, I invite you to act as an agent by finding them online or in Church publications. References are provided to guide you quickly to the sources.

My hope is that this book will cause you to ponder, pray, re-flect, evaluate, and act. May the combination of your faith in the Savior, your willingness to act as an agent, the text, and the learning experiences in which you will engage invite the Holy Ghost to help you more fully understand basic gospel truths and powerful spiritual patterns—to the end that each of us may *ACT IN DOCTRINE*.

CHAPTER ONE

ACTING IN DOCTRINE AND THE CHARACTER OF CHRIST

As we seek for the companionship of the Holy Ghost and strive faithfully to fulfill our personal responsibility to "increase in learning" (Proverbs 9:9), we more consistently "act in doctrine" (Doctrine and Covenants 101:78).

The word *act* denotes performing, behaving, and living. The doctrine of Christ is revealed truth that pertains to our eternal progression and happiness. Thus, to "act in doctrine" is to live according to and "in" revealed truth.

"But he that *doeth truth* cometh to the light, that his deeds may be made manifest, that they are wrought in God" (John 3:21; emphasis added).

"If any man will *do his will,* he shall know of the doctrine, whether it be of God, or whether I speak of myself" (John 7:17; emphasis added).

"Now this is the commandment: Repent, all ye ends of the earth, and come unto me and be baptized in my name, that ye may

1

be sanctified by the reception of the Holy Ghost, that ye may stand spotless before me at the last day.

"Verily, verily, I say unto you, this is my gospel; and ye know the things that ye must *do* in my church; for the works which ye have seen me *do* that shall ye also *do;* for that which ye have seen me *do* even that shall ye *do;*

"Therefore, if ye *do* these things blessed are ye, for ye shall be lifted up at the last day" (3 Nephi 27:20–22; emphasis added).

The process of effectively doing and living what we know to be true is one of the great challenges of mortality. Unfortunately for all of us, what we learn and know is not always reflected in what we do. As disciples of the Savior, we are not merely striving to know more; rather, we need to consistently do more of what we know is right and become better. "If ye know these things, happy are ye if ye do them" (John 13:17).

The scriptures repeatedly emphasize the important relationship between learning and doing.

"Learn of me, and listen to my words; *walk* in the meekness of my Spirit, and you shall have peace in me" (Doctrine and Covenants 19:23; emphasis added).

"O, remember, my son, and learn wisdom in thy youth; yea, *learn* in thy youth to *keep the commandments of God* (Alma 37:35; emphasis added).

"Wherefore, now let every man *learn his duty,* and to *act in the office* in which he is appointed, in all diligence" (Doctrine and Covenants 107:99; emphasis added).

"But *learn* that he who *doeth the works of righteousness* shall receive his reward, even peace in this world, and eternal life in the world to come" (Doctrine and Covenants 59:23; emphasis added).

"For immediately after I had *learned* these things of you I *inquired of the Lord* concerning the matter. And the word of the Lord came to me by the power of the Holy Ghost" (Moroni 8:7; emphasis added).

"And now concerning my servant Parley P. Pratt, behold, I say unto him that as I live I will that he shall declare my gospel and *learn* of me, and *be meek and lowly of heart*" (Doctrine and Covenants 32:1; emphasis added).

A simple question can provide a helpful starting point as we work to reduce the disparity between what we know and what we do. Given that true doctrine, understood, changes attitudes and behavior, then:

What doctrines and principles, *if understood*, would help me or you to live more consistently what we know is true?

As the first principle of the restored gospel is "faith in the Lord Jesus Christ" (Articles of Faith 1:4), we should begin at the beginning and learn about His nature and character as the Son of the living God. The answers always are in the doctrines and principles of His restored gospel.

The Character of Christ

Many years ago I participated in a training meeting at which Elder Neal A. Maxwell was the presiding authority. During the course of his teaching and testifying, Elder Maxwell made a statement that impressed me deeply. He said, "There would have been no Atonement except for the character of Christ."

After I returned home, this penetrating statement became a primary topic for my studying, reflecting, and praying. I read the New Testament and the Book of Mormon, repeatedly focusing upon the question, "What is the character of Christ?" I pondered. I sought to learn more about the word *character,* the relationship between Christ's character and the Atonement, and the implications of that relationship for each of us as disciples. And I discovered this relationship is central to understanding the responsibility each of us has to act in doctrine.

What Is Character?

The *Oxford English Dictionary* indicates that many of the uses of the word *character* relate to graphic symbols, printing, engraving, and writing. The usages I found most relevant, however, relate to "the sum of the moral and mental qualities which distinguish an individual or a race; mental or moral excellence and firmness; moral qualities strongly developed or strikingly displayed" (s.v. "Character"). Thus, *character* refers to the moral qualities of an individual that are conscientiously and consistently lived. Interestingly, the word *character* in the Topical Guide to the scriptures is cross-referenced to the topics of honesty, honor, and integrity.

Brigham Young emphasized the significance of the Savior's character as he testified about the truthfulness of the Holy Bible:

"The Bible is true. It may not all have been translated aright, and many precious things may have been rejected in the compilation and translation of the Bible; but we understand, from the writings of one of the Apostles, that if all the sayings and doings of the Savior had been written, the world could not contain them. I will say that the world could not understand them. They do not understand what we have on record, *nor the character of the Savior,* as delineated in the Scriptures" (*Discourses of Brigham Young,* 124, emphasis added).

Brigham Young further taught that faith must be focused upon Jesus' character, in His Atonement, and in the Father's plan of salvation:

"I will take the liberty of saying to every man and woman who wishes to obtain salvation through [the Savior] that looking to Him, only, is not enough: *they must have faith in His name, character and atonement;* and they must have faith in His Father and in the plan of salvation devised and wrought out by the Father and the Son. What will this faith lead to? It will lead to obedience to the requirements of the Gospel" (*Deseret News [Weekly],* July 28, 1869, 293; emphasis added).

The rock upon which we should build our spiritual foundation is our Redeemer and Savior. As Helaman taught his sons: "Remember, remember that it is upon the rock of our Redeemer, who is Christ, the Son of God, that ye must build your foundation; that when the devil shall send forth his mighty winds, yea, his shafts in the whirlwind, yea, when all his hail and his mighty storm shall beat upon you, it shall have no power over you to drag you down to the gulf of misery and endless wo, because of the rock upon which ye are built, which is a sure foundation, a foundation whereon if men build they cannot fall" (Helaman 5:12).

Jesus was the Firstborn of the Eternal Father, the Only Begotten Son in the flesh, the Redeemer of the world. Under the direction of His Father, He was the creator of the earth. He is the "Great I Am" (Doctrine and Covenants 29:1), Jehovah (Doctrine and Covenants 110:1–4), the God of ancient Israel who gave and fulfilled the law (3 Nephi 15:5), our advocate with the Father (Doctrine and Covenants 45:3–5), the one to whom the Father "hath committed all judgment" (John 5:22; see also Doctrine and Covenants 19:1–4), and the only "name under heaven given among men, whereby we must be saved" (Acts 4:12; see also 3 Nephi 27:3–10). Only through the Son can man come to the Father (see John 14:6–13).

Elder Bruce R. McConkie explained: "To gain salvation, men must come unto the Father, attain the faith that he exercises, and be as he is. Christ has done so; he is both a saved being and the perfect and only illustration of what others must do to gain like inheritances and be joint-heirs with him. He is thus the way to the Father; no man cometh unto the Father but by him and by his word. He is our Mediator, Advocate, and Intercessor, all because he wrought out the perfect atonement through the shedding of his own blood. Through him, and through him only, fallen men may be reconciled to God if they repent and work righteousness.

"Christ and his Father are one. They possess the same powers, are of the same character, embody the same attributes, and stand as beacons to all others with reference to the same eternal perfections. The words and acts of one are the words and acts of the other. The Father was in Christ manifesting himself to the world. Hence, faith in the Son is faith in the Father. And as Christ is the way to the Father, faith centers in him and in his redeeming sacrifice and goes thereby to the Father" (*A New Witness for the Articles of Faith,* 185).

As described in *Lectures on Faith,* one of the three things "necessary in order that any rational and intelligent being may exercise faith in [the Father and Son] unto life and salvation is a correct idea of [Their] character, perfections, and attributes" (page 33). Thus, the name, the character, and the Atonement of the Lord Jesus Christ lead us to the Father and are the basis for and ultimate source of a mighty change of heart (see Alma 5:12–14), of strong testimony, of deepening conversion, and of dedicated discipleship. To "increase in learning" (Proverbs 9:9–10) about the Savior's character is the essential first step if we are to reduce the gap between what we know and what we do, faithfully and more consistently "act in doctrine" (Doctrine and Covenants 101:78), receive the "power of his word . . . in us" (Alma 26:13), and truly "come unto Christ" (Moroni 10:32).

As you study and work through this chapter, please consider why a correct understanding of the Savior's character has an impact upon what and how we learn and how we act.

The Atonement and the Character of the Lord Jesus Christ

In a talk delivered to CES religious educators in February 1995, Elder Neal A. Maxwell specifically linked Christ's character to the infinite and eternal atoning sacrifice. This inspired message in general and the following excerpt in particular provided the doctrinal basis for his teaching in the training meeting that I referred to at the beginning of this chapter.

"Jesus' character necessarily underwrote His remarkable atonement. Without Jesus' sublime character there could have been no sublime atonement! His character is such that He '[suffered] temptations of every kind' (Alma 7:11), yet He gave temptations 'no heed' (D&C 20:22).

"Someone has said only those who resist temptation really understand the power of temptation. Because Jesus resisted it perfectly, He understood temptation perfectly: hence He can help us. The fact that He was dismissive of temptation and gave it 'no heed,' reveals His marvelous character, which we are to emulate (see D&C 20:22; 3 Nephi 12:48; 27:27)" ("O How Great the Plan of Our God," 5).

One of the greatest indicators of righteous character is the capacity to recognize and appropriately respond to other people who are experiencing the very challenge or adversity that is most immediately and forcefully pressing upon us. Character is revealed, for example, in the power to discern the suffering of other people when we ourselves are suffering; in the ability to detect the hunger of others when we are hungry; and in the power to reach out and extend compassion for the spiritual agony of others when we are in the midst of our own spiritual distress. Therefore, character is demonstrated by looking, turning, and reaching outward when the instinctive response of the "natural man" (Mosiah 3:19) in each of us is to turn inward and to be selfish and self-absorbed. And the Savior of the world is the source, the standard, and the ultimate criterion of moral character and the perfect example of charity and consistency.

See DVD Segment 5

Examples of Christ's Character in the New Testament

The New Testament is replete with "strikingly displayed" examples of the Savior's character.

Following His baptism by John the Baptist and as a preparation for His public ministry, the Savior fasted for forty days. He also was tempted by the adversary to use His supernal power inappropriately to satisfy physical desires by commanding that stones be made bread, to gain recognition by casting Himself down from the pinnacle of the temple, and to obtain wealth and power and prestige in exchange for falling down and worshipping the tempter (see Matthew 4:1–9).

The overarching and fundamental challenge to the Savior in each of these three temptations is summarized in the taunting statement, *"If thou be the Son of God."* Satan's objective, in essence, was to dare Jesus to turn inward, to use improperly His God-given powers, and thereby to betray His divine Sonship and identity. Thus, Satan attempted repeatedly to attack Jesus' understanding of who He was and of His relationship with His Father. Jesus was victorious in overcoming this strategy of Satan.

I suspect the Savior may have been at least partially spent physically after forty days of fasting—and somewhat drained spiritually after His encounter with the adversary. With this background information in mind, please consider the following verse from the New Testament.

"Then the devil leaveth him, and, behold, angels came and ministered unto him" (Matthew 4:11).

This scripture clearly indicates that angels came and ministered to the Savior after the devil had departed. And undoubtedly Jesus would have benefited from and been blessed by such a heavenly ministration in a time of physical and spiritual need. However, the Joseph Smith Translation of Matthew 4:11 provides a remarkable insight into the character of Christ. Please note the important differences in verse eleven between the King James Version and the Joseph Smith Translation.

"Then the devil leaveth him, and now Jesus knew that John

was cast into prison, and he sent angels, and, behold, they came and ministered unto him (John)" (JST, Matthew 4:11).

Importantly, the revisions found in the Joseph Smith Translation significantly enhance our understanding of this event and reveal the character of Christ—His righteous and moral qualities strongly developed and consistently lived. Angels did not come and minister to the Lord; rather, in His own state of spiritual, mental, and physical distress, He sent angels to minister to John the Baptist. Note that Jesus in the midst of His own challenge recognized and appropriately responded to John—who was experiencing a lesser challenge than that of the Savior. Consequently, the character of Christ was manifested as He reached outward and ministered to one who was suffering, even as He Himself was experiencing anguish and torment.

In similar circumstances, you and I as fallen, natural men and women would likely turn inward with self-absorption, self-pity, and selfishness. But the character of Christ, the consistent capacity to turn outward and minister to others in the midst of affliction, is the very foundation of the infinite and eternal atoning sacrifice.

In the upper room on the night of the Last Supper, the precise night during which He would experience the greatest suffering ever to occur in all of the worlds created by Him under the direction of the Father, Christ spoke about the Comforter and peace.

"These things have I spoken unto you, being yet present with you.

"But the Comforter, which is the Holy Ghost, whom the Father will send in my name, he shall teach you all things, and bring all things to your remembrance, whatsoever I have said unto you.

"Peace I leave with you, my peace I give unto you: not as the world giveth, give I unto you. Let not your heart be troubled, neither let it be afraid" (John 14:25–27).

The fundamental character of Christ is again revealed magnificently in this tender incident. Recognizing that He Himself was about to experience intensely and personally the absence of both comfort and peace, and in a moment when His heart was perhaps troubled, the Master reached outward and offered to others the very blessings that could and would have strengthened Him. He prayed for comfort and peace for others, not for Himself.

In the great Intercessory Prayer, offered immediately before Jesus went forth with His disciples over the brook Cedron to the Garden of Gethsemane, the Master prayed for His disciples and for all "which shall believe on me through their word;

"That they all may be one; as thou, Father, art in me, . . . that they may be made perfect in one; and that the world may know that thou hast sent me, and hast loved them, as thou hast loved me. . . .

"And I have declared unto them thy name, and will declare it: that the love wherewith thou hast loved me may be in them, and I in them" (John 17:20–21, 23, 26).

I repeatedly ask myself the following questions as I ponder this and other events that took place so close to the Savior's betrayal and suffering in the garden: How could He pray for the well-being and unity of others immediately before His own anguish? What enabled Him to seek comfort and peace for those whose need was so much less than His? As the fallen nature of the world He had created pressed in upon Him, how could He focus so totally and so exclusively upon the conditions and concerns of others? How was the Master able to reach outward when a lesser being would have turned inward? Again, the powerful statement from Elder Maxwell provides the answer to each of these questions:

"Jesus' character necessarily underwrote His remarkable atonement. Without Jesus' sublime character there could have been no sublime atonement! His character is such that He '[suffered] temptations of every kind' (Alma 7:11), yet He gave temptations 'no heed' (D&C 20:22)" ("O How Great the Plan of Our God," 5).

Jesus, who suffered the most, has the most compassion for all of us who suffer so much less. In the Garden of Gethsemane, Jesus bore the sins, the inequity, the infirmities, and sicknesses, and the pains of all mankind for all time and all eternity (see Alma 7:11–12). He sweat great drops of blood from every pore as He suffered to meet the demands of the eternal law of justice (see Doctrine and Covenants 19:18; Mosiah 3:7; Alma 42:15). Consider the scene as the Redeemer emerged from His awful agony and encountered a multitude.

"And while he yet spake, behold a multitude, and he that was called Judas, one of the twelve, went before them, and drew near unto Jesus to kiss him.

"But Jesus said unto him, Judas, betrayest thou the Son of man with a kiss?

"When they which were about him saw what would follow, they said unto him, Lord, shall we smite with the sword?

"And one of them smote the servant of the high priest, and cut off his right ear" (Luke 22:47–50).

Given the magnitude and intensity of Jesus' agony in the garden, His sorrow that His chief Apostles were unable to watch with Him one hour (see Matthew 26:38–46), and the heartache of betrayal by one of His Apostles (see Matthew 26:47–50), it perhaps would have been understandable if He had not noticed and attended to the guard's severed ear. But the Savior's character activated a compassion that was perfect. Note His response to the guard's injury.

"And Jesus answered and said, Suffer ye thus far. And he touched his ear, and healed him" (Luke 22:51).

The Savior used His supernal powers to restore the guard's ear—a demonstration of His divinity He never would employ for Himself (review again Matthew 4:1–9). Thus, the character of Christ is to turn outward in compassion and service when facing spiritual adversity or physical pain even as the natural man in each of us would turn inward in self-obsession and self-interest.

As individually impressive as is each of the preceding events, I believe it is the consistency of the Lord's character across multiple episodes that is ultimately the most instructive and inspiring. In addition to the incidents we have reviewed thus far, recall how, as the Lord was taken to Calvary and the awful agony of the Crucifixion was commenced, He pleaded with the Father to "forgive them; for they know not what they do" (Luke 23:34).

Consider how Jesus, while hanging on the cross, instructed the Apostle John about caring for His mother, Mary (see John 19:26–27).

Remember also that in the midst of excruciating spiritual and physical pain, the Savior reassured one of the thieves on the cross, "To day shalt thou be with me in paradise" (Luke 23:43).

Throughout His mortal ministry, and especially during the events leading up to and including the atoning sacrifice, the Savior of the world turned outward—when the natural man or woman in most of us would have focused inward.

Developing a Christlike Character

We can in mortality seek to be blessed with and develop essential elements of a Christlike character. Indeed, it is possible for us as mortals to strive in righteousness to receive the spiritual gifts associated with the capacity to reach outward and appropriately respond to other people who are experiencing the very challenge or adversity that is most immediately and forcefully pressing upon us. We cannot obtain such a capacity through sheer willpower or personal determination. Rather, we need and are dependent upon "the merits, and mercy, and grace of the Holy Messiah" (2 Nephi 2:8). But "line upon line, precept upon precept" (2 Nephi 28:30) and in the process of time (see Moses 7:21), we can increasingly reach outward when the natural tendency is for us to turn inward.

The letters *A, C,* and *T* comprise a central element of the word char**ACT**er. As we already have seen in the examples of Christ's strongly developed, strikingly displayed, and consistently lived character in the New Testament, the nature and constancy of how one **act**s reveals in a powerful way his or her true char**act**er. Two memorable experiences from my service as a stake president highlight the relationship between acting in doctrine as disciples and obtaining a Christlike character.

Early one summer morning, I received a phone call from a dear sister and friend informing me of a tragic automobile accident that had just occurred involving three teenage girls from our stake. Our friend indicated that one of the young women had already been pronounced dead at the scene of the accident and the other two were badly injured and presently were being transported to a regional medical center. She further reported that the identity of the deceased young woman was not yet known. There was urgency in her voice, but there was no panic or excessive alarm. She then asked if I could go to the hospital, meet the ambulance when it arrived, and assist in identifying the young women. I answered that I would leave immediately.

During the course of our telephone conversation, as I listened to both the information being conveyed and the voice of our friend, I gradually became aware of two important things. First, this friend's daughter was one of the young women involved in the accident. Our friend lived approximately thirty-five miles from the hospital and therefore needed the assistance of someone who lived closer to the city. Second, I detected that the mother was using two telephone handsets simultaneously—one pressed to each of her ears. I became aware that as she was talking with me, she was also talking with a nurse at a small rural hospital who had initially attended to the three accident victims. Our friend was receiving updated information about the condition of the young women in the very moment she was informing me about the accident and requesting my help. I then heard one of the most remarkable things I have ever heard in my life.

I faintly heard the nurse telling this faithful mother and friend that the young woman pronounced dead at the scene of the accident had been positively identified as her daughter. I could not believe what I was hearing. I was listening to this good woman in the very moment that she learned of the death of her precious daughter. Without hesitation, and with a calm and most deliberate voice, our friend next said, "President Bednar, we must get in contact with the two other mothers. We must let them know as much as we can about the condition of their daughters and that they will soon be admitted into the hospital."

The Christlike character of this devoted woman was manifested in her immediate and almost instinctive turning outward to attend to the needs of other suffering mothers. There was no self-pity; there was no self-absorption; there was no turning inward. It was a moment and a lesson that I have never forgotten. At a time of ultimate grief, this dear friend reached outward when I likely would have turned inward.

I drove to the hospital with concern in my heart for the

well-being of the two other beautiful young women who had been involved in the accident. Little did I realize that the lessons I would learn about Christlike character—lessons taught by seemingly ordinary disciples—were just beginning.

I arrived at the hospital and proceeded to the emergency room. After properly establishing who I was and my relationship to the victims, I was invited into two different treatment areas to identify the injured young women. It was obvious that their respective wounds were serious and life threatening. And the lovely countenances and physical features of these young women had been badly marred. Within a relatively short period of time, the two remaining young women died. All three of these virtuous, lovely, and engaging young women—who seemed to have so much of life in front of them—suddenly had been called home to their Heavenly Father.

My attention and the attention of the respective families then shifted to funeral arrangements and logistics. A day or so later, in the midst of program planning and detail arranging for the three funerals, I received a phone call from a ward Relief Society president. This faithful woman was a single mother rearing her only child, and that daughter had been one of the victims in the accident. She and I had talked several times about her desires for the funeral program. I was especially close to this woman and her daughter, having served as both their bishop and their stake president.

After reviewing and finalizing several details for the funeral of her daughter, this good sister said to me, "President, I am sure it was difficult for you to see my daughter in the emergency room the other day. She was severely injured and disfigured. As you know, we are not going to have an open casket at the viewing. I have just returned from the funeral home, and they have helped my daughter to look so lovely again. I was just wondering—why don't we arrange a time when we can meet at the mortuary and you can have one last look at her before she is buried? Then your final memories of my daughter will not be the images you saw in the emergency room."

I listened and marveled at the compassion and thoughtfulness this sister had for me. Her only daughter had just been tragically killed, but she was concerned about the potentially troublesome memories I might have, given my experience in the emergency room. In this good woman I detected no self-pity and no turning inward. Sorrow, certainly. Sadness, absolutely. Nevertheless, she reached outward when many or perhaps most of us would have turned inward with sorrow and grief.

On the day of her daughter's funeral, this Relief Society president received a phone call from an irritated sister in her ward who evidently did not know about the deaths of the three young women. The complaining sister did not feel well, and she caustically berated the Relief Society president for not being thoughtful or compassionate enough to arrange for meals to be delivered to her home. Time and circumstances made delegating the task complicated, so, just hours before the funeral of her only child, this remarkable woman and disciple prepared and delivered a meal to the grumbling sister.

We appropriately and rightly speak with reverence and awe of young men who sacrificed their lives to rescue stranded handcart pioneers—and of other mighty men and women who repeatedly gave their all to establish the Church in the early days of the Restoration. I have equal reverence and awe for these two mothers—women of faith and conversion and character—who taught me so much and instinctively reached outward when most of us

See DVD Segment 13

would have turned inward. Oh, how I appreciate their quiet and powerful examples!

The exceptional examples of these two stalwart women, who "in process of time" (Moses 7:21) had been blessed to receive the spiritual gifts and capacity that constitute a portion of the character of Christ, may cause some of us to conclude that we simply have not progressed far enough along the strait and narrow path (see 2 Nephi 33:9) to act as they did in response to such tragedy and heartache. But as we do our best to "press forward with a steadfastness in Christ, having a perfect brightness of hope, and a love of God and of all men" (2 Nephi 31:20), then we are blessed to do and to become much more than perhaps we are able to recognize. The Lord's pattern for spiritual development is "line upon line, precept upon precept, here a little and there a little" (2 Nephi 28:30)—gradual, steady, and incremental progress over time. I frankly do not think these two remarkable sisters would have thought before the terrible accident that they could react as they did. What those women had become and were becoming through the Savior's grace was revealed and "strikingly displayed" in a moment of great adversity.

But how had those women progressed to such a point? We can learn much about the nature and importance of this line-upon-line pattern of spiritual development from the technique of drip irrigation that is used in many gardens and in agricultural areas throughout the world.

Drip irrigation, sometimes called trickle irrigation, involves dripping water onto the soil at very low rates from a system of small plastic pipes fitted with outlets called emitters or drippers. Unlike surface and sprinkler irrigation that involves flooding or gushing or spraying large quantities of water where it may not be needed, drip irrigation applies water close to a plant so that only the part of the soil in which the roots grow is wetted. With drip irrigation, applications of water are more focused and more frequent than with the other methods. The steady drips of water sink deep into the ground and provide a high moisture level in the soil wherein plants can flourish.

In like manner, if you and I are focused and frequent in receiving consistent drops of spiritual nourishment, then gospel roots can sink deep into our soul, can become firmly established and grounded, and can produce extraordinary and delicious fruit.

See DVD Segment 4

This spiritual pattern produces firmness and steadfastness, deepening devotion, and more complete development of a Christlike character. As you and I become increasingly steadfast and immovable, we are less prone to zealous and exaggerated spurts of spirituality followed by extended periods of slackness. A spiritual "spurter" is one who is given to a short burst of spectacular effort followed by frequent and lengthy periods of rest.

A big spurt may appear to be impressive in the short run, but steadiness in small things over time is far more effective, far less dangerous, and produces far better results. Three consecutive days of fasting ultimately will not be as spiritually efficacious as three successive months of appropriate fasting and worship on the designated fast Sunday—of many small and simple things done consistently well. A great attempt to pray one time for five hours likely will not produce the spiritual results of meaningful morning and evening prayer offered consistently over five weeks or five months—of many small and simple things done consistently well. And a single, great scripture-reading marathon cannot produce the spiritual impact of steady scripture study across many months.

As we work to develop a Christlike character, we will discover that "by small and simple things are great things brought to pass" (Alma 37:6).

One final example, this one from my experience as a father, emphasizes the impact of the character of Christ in the seemingly ordinary and routine activities of our daily lives—and how we should "be not weary in well-doing, for ye are laying the foundation of a great work. And out of small things proceedeth that which is great" (Doctrine and Covenants 64:33).

One of our sons and I were assigned as home teaching companions. Together we taught a number of families, including a divorced sister with three young daughters. Over time we developed a close and trusting relationship with the woman and her children. We appreciated the opportunities we had to serve them spiritually and temporally.

I was privileged to give each of the daughters a priesthood blessing at the beginning of every new school year, a cherished spiritual tradition both for the young women and for my son and me. Shortly after my son received the Melchizedek Priesthood and was ordained to the office of an elder, we were scheduled to visit the home of this good sister and her daughters. It was the time of the year for "back to school" blessings, and in our planning for the appointment I invited our son to be the voice in giving one of the blessings. We reviewed what he already knew about the pattern for priesthood blessings. He was both excited and a bit nervous about his first opportunity to exercise the higher priesthood "by the laying on of hands" (Articles of Faith 1:5).

After we presented a spiritual lesson to and talked with the family, I asked if all were ready to receive their blessings. With the concurrence of the mother, I invited our son to first bless the oldest daughter. He did an admirable job and was appropriate and inspired in his utterances.

Upon the completion of the first blessing, I looked at our son and invited him to give a blessing to the second daughter. This request was a total surprise to him! My son looked at me with an expression of semi-terror only a dad could interpret, a look that silently screamed, *What are you doing? Please do not ask me to do this. I already used all of the standard phrases I know. I do not know what else to say. Just let me watch and listen to you.*

Throughout his life this worthy and valiant young man had received and observed scores of priesthood blessings. But the immediate challenge for him now was to translate, with the help of the Lord, what he knew in his mind and heart into priesthood power and action. I politely but persistently invited him a second time to give the blessing, and he responded in faith. The tone and spirit of the second blessing were different from the first—more humble, more submissive, and more earnest. He clearly received heavenly help beyond his own power as he labored to be a conduit through whom the Lord could reveal His mind and will.

As the third young woman came forward to sit in the chair in the middle of the living room, I invited our son to be the voice for the third blessing. This request also was a total surprise to him. The look of panic and protest in his eyes was now gone, and he placed his hands upon the young woman's head, paused, and then began to speak. The third blessing was different from the first two—more individualized, more penetrating, and more soothing. Customary phrases were replaced by light and truth. Both the receiver and the giver of the blessing were edified and rejoiced together (see Doctrine and Covenants 50:17–26), and all of us in that home that evening felt the power of the Holy Ghost.

As we drove home, my son and I talked about what he had experienced, observed, felt, and learned. During the first blessing, he had been worried and concerned about himself: about how *he* was doing; about how *his* blessing was being received and understood; and about whether *he* was following the proper priesthood pattern and protocol. While giving the second blessing, he began to "get out of the way." He focused less upon himself and more upon the needs and concerns of the young woman, upon the impressions of the Spirit, and upon the Lord's will. And in the third blessing, he increasingly had "an eye single to the glory of God, [which qualified] him for the work" (Doctrine and Covenants 4:5). He learned about the power of the priesthood more deeply and intensely in those few minutes of "acting in doctrine" than he had learned in all of the previous priesthood lessons he had ever received or blessings he had observed.

That initial experience of giving blessings in the authority of the Melchizedek Priesthood enabled that young man to become acquainted with the character of Christ as perhaps nothing else could. Our son had repeatedly heard, read, studied, taught, and learned the doctrine of the priesthood. But only as he acted in the doctrine did he start to make the transformational turn from inward to outward—from self to others. Only as he acted in doctrine could what he knew in his mind begin to find place in his heart. Only as he acted in doctrine would he more fully understand Him whom he represented and whose authority he now bore.

I noted earlier in this chapter that the letters *A, C,* and *T* form a central component in the word char**act**er. Also noteworthy is the similarity between the words **char**acter and **char**ity—as both words contain the letters *C, H, A,* and *R.* Etymologically there is no relationship between these two words. Nevertheless, I believe several conceptual connections are important to consider and ponder.

Let me suggest that you and I must be praying and yearning and striving and working to cultivate a Christlike **char**acter if we hope to receive the spiritual gift of **char**ity—the pure love of Christ. Charity is not a trait or characteristic we acquire exclusively through our own purposive persistence and determination. Indeed we must honor our covenants and live worthily and do all that we can do to qualify for the gift, but ultimately the gift of charity possesses us—we do not possess it.

"Wherefore, my beloved brethren, if ye have not charity, ye are nothing, for charity never faileth. Wherefore, cleave unto charity, which is the greatest of all, for all things must fail—But charity is the pure love of Christ, and it endureth forever; and whoso is found *possessed of it* at the last day, it shall be well with him" (Moroni 7:46–47; emphasis added).

The Lord determines if and when we receive all spiritual gifts, but we must do all in our power to desire and yearn after and invite and qualify for such gifts. As we increasingly **act** in the doctrine of Christ and in a manner congruent with His **charact**er, then perhaps we are indicating to heaven in a most powerful manner our desire for the supernal spiritual gift of **char**ity. And clearly we are being blessed with this marvelous gift as we increasingly reach outward when the natural man or woman in us would naturally turn inward.

It requires faith to act upon the promptings we receive to turn outward, especially when the reasons for those promptings are not immediately apparent. Some time ago I spoke with a priesthood leader who was prompted to memorize the names of all of the youth ages thirteen to twenty-one in his stake. Using snapshots of the young men and women, he created flash cards that he reviewed while traveling on business and at other times. This priesthood leader quickly learned all of the names of the youth.

One night the priesthood leader had a dream about one of the young men whom he knew only from a picture. In the dream he saw the young man dressed in a white shirt and wearing a missionary name tag. With a companion seated at his side, the young man

NOTES

See DVD Segment 12

was teaching a family. The young man held the Book of Mormon in his hand, and he looked as if he were testifying of the truthfulness of the book. The priesthood leader then awoke from his dream.

At an ensuing priesthood gathering, the leader approached the young man he had seen in his dream and asked to talk with him for a few minutes. After a brief introduction, the leader called the young man by name and said: "I am not a dreamer. I have never had a dream about a single member of this stake, except for you. I am going to tell you about my dream, and then I would like you to help me understand what it means."

The priesthood leader recounted the dream and asked the young man about its meaning. Choking with emotion, the young man simply replied, "It means God knows who I am." The remainder of the conversation between this young man and his priesthood leader was most meaningful, and they agreed to meet and counsel together from time to time during the following months.

That young man received the Lord's tender mercies through an inspired priesthood leader who turned outward from his own concerns to gain a greater acquaintance with the youth whom he served. Similarly, as we develop the character of Christ and act in doctrine, we become His agents in performing His work among His sons and daughters.

This chapter concludes by returning to where it began—the statement by Elder Maxwell about the relationship between the Savior's character and the Atonement: "There would have been no Atonement except for the character of Christ." Through our study of the Lord's life, we can more fully come unto Him, more completely become like Him, and more fervently worship, reverence, and adore Him. And through His merits, mercy, and grace (see 2 Nephi 2:8) and in His strength (see Mosiah 9:17; Mosiah 10:10;

Alma 20:4), we can receive help to reduce the disparity in our discipleship between what we know of and about Him and what we do as we follow Him.

Summary

Nephi, the elder son of Helaman, proclaimed that "as many as should look upon the Son of God with faith, having a contrite spirit, might live, even unto that life which is eternal" (Helaman 8:15). This verse primarily focuses upon the blessing of eternal life made possible through the Atonement of Jesus Christ and faith upon His name.

But this scripture also emphasizes how we "might live" in mortality—a life of obedience, devotion, conversion, and consecration—by coming unto Christ and being perfected in Him (see Moroni 10:32). Such a life is lived "even unto that life which is eternal."

As we strive to have "this mind be in [us], which was also in Christ Jesus" (Philippians 2:5), we readily recognize that what we know about the Savior and His restored gospel is not always reflected in what we do and how we live. And the essential first step in reducing the disparity between gospel knowledge and righteous behavior is learning about and emulating the character of Christ.

If as disciples we are to exercise faith unto salvation, we first must have a correct idea of the character, perfections, and attributes of the Father and the Son.

And as we learn of Christ we learn of the Father. The Master's capacity to turn outward and minister to others in the midst of His own affliction "marked the path and led the way" ("How Great the Wisdom and the Love," *Hymns,* no. 195) whereby we can during our mortal probation put off the selfish tendencies of the natural man, more consistently act in true doctrine, and "[become] a saint through the atonement of Christ the Lord" (Mosiah 3:19)—even unto that life which is eternal.

Related Readings for Chapter One

The two related readings for Chapter One highlight the importance of exercising our moral agency to act in accordance with the teachings of the gospel of Jesus Christ. As we so live, we are blessed over time to obtain an increasing measure of the character of Christ.

"The Tender Mercies of the Lord"
Ensign, May 2005, 99–102

We invite the Lord's tender mercies into our lives as we choose God and love and serve one another. You and I ultimately determine through our decisions and actions if we are prepared to receive and recognize these supernal blessings in our lives.

"Ask in Faith"
Ensign, May 2008, 94–97

Joseph Smith is the perfect example of one of the key elements of meaningful prayer—asking in faith with the expectation to act. And coming to accept and submit to God's will through sincere prayer is essential in emulating the Savior.

CONSIDER

What can and should I do to ensure my faith is centered on the Savior's name, character, and Atonement?

CONSIDER

Why does increasing my understanding of the character of Christ help to reduce the disparity between what I know and what I do?

CONSIDER

What can and should I do in my life to continue turning away from selfishness and toward Christlike compassion and selfless service?

My Own Questions to Consider

Scriptures Related to What I Am Learning

SCRIPTURES RELATED TO WHAT I AM LEARNING

AN INVITATION TO LEARN AND ACT		
What additional doctrines and principles, if understood, would help me to obtain appropriately a greater measure of the character of Christ?	What can and should I do to "act in" those doctrines and principles?	How will I know if I am making progress in striving to become more like the Savior?

AN INVITATION TO LEARN AND ACT		
What additional doctrines and principles, if understood, would help me to obtain appropriately a greater measure of the character of Christ?	What can and should I do to "act in" those doctrines and principles?	How will I know if I am making progress in striving to become more like the Savior?

AN INVITATION TO LEARN AND ACT		
What additional doctrines and principles, if understood, would help me to obtain appropriately a greater measure of the character of Christ?	What can and should I do to "act in" those doctrines and principles?	How will I know if I am making progress in striving to become more like the Savior?

CHAPTER TWO

ACTING IN DOCTRINE AND MORAL AGENCY

The gift of moral agency is a central element in the Father's plan of happiness and a supernal blessing. Agency is the source of our capacity to "act in doctrine."

"That every man may act in doctrine and principle pertaining to futurity, *according to the moral agency which I have given unto him,* that every man may be accountable for his own sins in the day of judgment" (Doctrine and Covenants 101:78; emphasis added).

The importance of moral agency cannot be overemphasized. President Boyd K. Packer explained:

"If you put all of the doctrines of the Church in boxes and laid them on a large floor and asked me to assemble them in some order, I would sort through the boxes and find one. It would be a long box and a heavy one, and it would say 'Agency, Freedom, Agency.' I would put that down first, and everything else we believe would be stacked in proper order on top of that" (*Mine Errand from the Lord,* 176).

Thus, agency is the fundamental foundation upon which all other gospel doctrines and principles rest.

Moral Agency and the Premortal Council

In the premortal council, our Heavenly Father presented to His spirit sons and daughters His plan for their eternal progression and happiness.

"We will go down, for there is space there, and we will take of these materials, and we will make an earth whereon these may dwell;

"And we will prove them herewith, to see if they will do all things whatsoever the Lord their God shall command them;

"And they who keep their first estate shall be added upon; and they who keep not their first estate shall not have glory in the same kingdom with those who keep their first estate; and they who keep their second estate shall have glory added upon their heads for ever and ever.

"And the Lord said: Whom shall I send? And one answered like unto the Son of Man: Here am I, send me. And another answered and said: Here am I, send me. And the Lord said: I will send the first.

"And the second was angry, and kept not his first estate; and, at that day, many followed after him" (Abraham 3:24–28).

Note that only one plan was presented in the premortal council—the Father's plan. Our Heavenly Father did not pose the question, "What shall we do?" He did not seek input, solicit recommendations, or request proposals. Rather, He presented the basic elements of His plan and asked, "Whom shall I send?" The essence of His question focused upon who should be sent to execute the terms and conditions of His plan.

Lucifer's Rebellion

The first to answer the question posed by Heavenly Father was Jesus Christ; the second was Lucifer. Additional details about the two respondents and their replies to the Father's question were revealed to Moses.

"And I, the Lord God, spake unto Moses, saying: That Satan, whom thou hast commanded in the name of mine Only Begotten, is the same which was from the beginning, and he came before me, saying—Behold, here am I, send me, I will be thy son, and I will redeem all mankind, that one soul shall not be lost, and surely I will do it; wherefore give me thine honor.

"But, behold, my Beloved Son, which was my Beloved and Chosen from the beginning, said unto me—Father, thy will be done, and the glory be thine forever" (Moses 4:1–2).

See DVD Segment 11

These verses show a stark contrast between the nature and character of the Savior versus the nature and character of Lucifer. The statement of Jesus includes no references to Himself. Before the foundation of the earth and from the beginning of time, Jesus humbly turned outward, desired to do the will of the Father, and wanted only to bring glory to Him. The Lord's willingness to submit to God's will and offer Himself as the infinite and eternal atoning sacrifice (see Alma 34:10) preserved moral agency in mortality for Heavenly Father's spirit children. Thus, as sons and daughters of God we are *agents* with the inherent capacity to act and to learn—and not *objects* that primarily are acted upon (see 2 Nephi 2:26).

Satan, on the other hand, turned inward, desired to achieve his own selfish interests, and wanted to usurp the glory of the Father for himself. The rebellious declaration of the devil uses the words

I or *me* six times in a sentence of thirty-five words. The adversary's desire was that we as learners would only be acted upon.

The consequences of the adversary's insurrection also are described in the scriptures.

"Wherefore, because that Satan rebelled against me, *and sought to destroy the agency of man,* which I, the Lord God, had given him, and also, that I should give unto him mine own power; by the power of mine Only Begotten, I caused that he should be cast down;

"And he became Satan, yea, even the devil, the father of all lies, to deceive and to blind men, and to lead them captive at his will, even as many as would not hearken unto my voice" (Moses 4:3–4; emphasis added).

Please remember that Lucifer did not present a plan that subsequently was voted down by a majority of the participants in the premortal council. He was not a sympathetic figure who lost a close election. He was a malcontent who rebelled! Selfishness, pride, and arrogance motivated his revolt against the Father's plan.

The adversary's intent was to negate agency. If agency were nullified, then no sins or transgressions ever would have been committed by the sons and daughters of God—no fall of Adam and no individual sins. If no sins or transgressions were committed, then the law of justice would not be violated. And if the law of justice were not violated, then there would be no need for a redeeming sacrifice to meet the demands of the law.

Lucifer sought for the glory of the Father without a willingness to abide by the law of the harvest (see Galatians 6:7) and pay the price. He had absolutely no concern for or interest in our welfare; he only wanted to use us to get something for himself. The selfish strategy he employed in the premortal council was the first "something for nothing" scam ever attempted.

The devil's premortal actions speak volumes about who he is, what he wants, and how he works. Satan is impatient, impulsive, impetuous, and intolerant—and "he seeketh that all men might be miserable like unto himself" (2 Nephi 2:27).

To Act and Not Be Acted Upon

Elder Marion G. Romney explained that mortality without agency would relegate men and women to be "puppets in the hands of fate" and "there would be no existence." For this reason, the protection of agency "is more important than the preservation of life" (in Conference Report, October 1968, 65).

The role of agency in empowering men and women to become much more than "puppets in the hands of fate" (see 2 Nephi 2:26) and to avoid having "no existence" (see 2 Nephi 2:11–13) is powerfully demonstrated in the experiences and observations of Dr. Viktor Frankl, an Austrian neurologist, psychiatrist, and World War II concentration camp survivor. His best-selling book, *Man's Search for Meaning,* details his experiences as a camp inmate and highlights the importance of agency in avoiding and overcoming the misery the adversary hopes will be our reward.

"The experiences of camp life show that man does have a choice of action. There were enough examples, often of a heroic nature, which proved that apathy could be overcome, irritability suppressed. Man *can* preserve a vestige of spiritual freedom, of independence of mind, even in such terrible conditions of psychic and physical stress.

"We who lived in concentration camps can remember the men who walked through the huts comforting others, giving away their last piece of bread. They may have been few in number, but they offer sufficient proof that everything can be taken from a man but one thing: the last of the human freedoms—to choose one's at-titude in any given set of circumstances, to choose one's own way.

"Even though conditions such as lack of sleep, insufficient food and various mental stresses may suggest that the inmates were bound to react in certain ways, in the final analysis it becomes clear that the sort of person the prisoner became was the result of an inner decision, and not the result of camp influences alone. Fundamentally, therefore, any man can, even under such circumstances, decide what shall become of him—mentally and spiritually. He may retain his human dignity even in a concentration camp. . . . I became acquainted with those martyrs whose behavior in camp, whose suffering and death, bore witness to the fact that the last inner freedom cannot be lost. . . .

"The way in which a man accepts his fate and all the suffering it entails, the way in which he takes up his cross, gives him ample opportunity—even in the most difficult circumstances—to add a deeper meaning to life" (*Man's Search for Meaning*, 65–67).

These observations by Dr. Frankl powerfully affirm the eternal truth that sons and daughters of God, blessed with moral agency, are agents with the capacity and power to act and are not merely objects to be acted upon (see 2 Nephi 2:26).

COVENANTS AND MORAL AGENCY

A covenant is an agreement between God and His children upon the earth, and it is important to recognize that God determines the conditions of all gospel covenants. You and I do not select or choose the elements of a covenant. Rather, exercising our moral agency, we accept the terms and requirements of a covenant as our Eternal Father has established them (see Bible Dictionary, s.v. "Covenant," 651).

Covenants and Turning to God

The act of exercising agency and entering into a covenant with God—for example, the covenant associated with the ordinance of baptism—commences a gradual and eternally important transformation. As we turn to the Savior and away from selfishness and sin, we start to "[put] off the natural man" (Mosiah 3:19).

"But if ye will *turn to the Lord* with full purpose of heart, and put your trust in him, and serve him with all diligence of mind, if ye do this, he will, according to his own will and pleasure, deliver you out of bondage" (Mosiah 7:33; emphasis added).

"Therefore also now, saith the Lord, *turn ye even to me* with all your heart, and with fasting, and with weeping, and with mourning:

"And rend your heart, and not your garments, and *turn unto the Lord your God:* for he is gracious and merciful, slow to anger, and of great kindness" (Joel 2:12–13; emphasis added).

"O repent ye, repent ye! Why will ye die? *Turn* ye, *turn* ye unto the Lord your God" (Helaman 7:17; emphasis added).

"But if ye will repent and *return unto the Lord your God* I will turn away mine anger, saith the Lord; yea, thus saith the Lord, blessed are they who will repent and *turn* unto me, but wo unto him that repenteth not" (Helaman 13:11; emphasis added).

We begin the process of becoming a saint (see Mosiah 3:19) by humbly emulating and striving to obtain the character of Christ as we turn to obedience and righteousness, deny ourselves, take up His cross, and follow Him (see Matthew 16:24; Mark 8:34; Luke 9:23).

"And we are willing to enter into a covenant with our God to do his will, and to be obedient to his commandments in all things that he shall command us, all the remainder of our days, that we may not bring upon ourselves a never-ending torment, as has been spoken by the angel, that we may not drink out of the cup of the wrath of God. . . .

"And now, because of the covenant which ye have made ye shall be called the children of Christ, his sons, and his daughters; for behold, this day he hath spiritually begotten you; for ye say that your hearts are changed through faith on his name; therefore, ye are born of him and have become his sons and his daughters.

"And under this head ye are made free, and there is no other head whereby ye can be made free. There is no other name given whereby salvation cometh; therefore, I would that ye should take upon you the name of Christ, all you that have entered into the covenant with God that ye should be obedient unto the end of your lives" (Mosiah 5:5, 7–8).

As we enter into, remember, and honor sacred covenants, we experience the Savior's character more fully and are blessed with increased freedom and capacity to act in accordance with His teachings. What we know increasingly becomes a part of who we are and what we do.

Binding Ourselves to Act in All Holiness

As we turn to the Savior and away from self through covenants, we in essence bind ourselves to act in doctrine.

"And now, behold, I give unto you a commandment, that when ye are assembled together ye shall instruct and edify each other, that ye may know how to act and direct my church, how to act upon the points of my law and commandments, which I have given.

"And thus ye shall become instructed in the law of my church, and be sanctified by that which ye have received, and *ye shall bind yourselves to act in all holiness before me*—

"That inasmuch as ye do this, glory shall be added to the kingdom which ye have received. Inasmuch as ye do it not, it shall be taken, even that which ye have received" (Doctrine and Covenants 43:8–10; emphasis added).

The word *bind* is instructive and suggests fastening tightly, tying together, and securing. Hands that are bound have no slack or wiggle room.

The earth was created and prepared as a place whereon Heavenly Father's children could be proved to see if they would do "*all things* whatsoever the Lord their God shall command them" (Abraham 3:25; emphasis added). The very purposes of the Creation and of our mortal existence are to see if you and I will do and become what the Lord instructs and commands us to do and to become. We have not been blessed with moral agency to do whatever we want whenever we will. Rather, according to the Father's plan, we have received moral agency to choose the right, to do good, and to become whatever God intends for us to become.

The Lord instructed Enoch on this precise point of doctrine:

"Behold these thy brethren; they are the workmanship of mine own hands, and I gave unto them their knowledge, in the day I created them; and in the Garden of Eden, gave I unto man his agency;

"And unto thy brethren have I said, and also given commandment, that they should love one another, and that they should choose me, their Father" (Moses 7:32–33).

As we learn in these scriptures, the fundamental purposes for the gift of agency are to love one another and to choose God. Note that we are commanded—not admonished, not urged, and not counseled, but *commanded*—to use our agency to turn outward, to love one another, and to choose God. For this purpose the earth was created. For this purpose you and I are here in the second estate. For this purpose we were blessed with the gift of moral agency.

During my service as the president of Brigham Young University–Idaho, I had many opportunities to talk with students about the honor and dress codes. Sometimes students would ask why it was necessary to have the codes and whether such guidelines imposed inappropriate restrictions on their agency. "Should we not have more freedom to choose how we will act and dress?" the young people would ask.

In response to such questions, I typically explained to students that they were totally free to act and dress in any way they desired—but not while enrolled at the university. A few of the young people seemed to believe the institution was imposing restrictions upon them; they failed to understand that their choice to attend the university precluded some styles of dress and types of behavior.

I often posed several questions for the young people to consider as a way of helping them remember the commitment they had made and the obligation they had assumed.

• As you reviewed information about and applied for admission to the university, did you learn about the honor and dress codes?

• Did you understand adequately the key provisions of the honor and dress codes?

• As you were accepted for admission into the university, do you remember reading and signing your commitment to abide by the honor and dress codes?

If the answer to each of the questions was yes, I indicated to the students they had exercised their agency in accepting the commitment to live according to the basic terms of the honor and dress codes. In essence, they had relinquished the freedom to act without consequences. Having acted as individual agents in making the decision, they did "bind" themselves and were duty bound to honor the commitment. And as a result of that responsibility, they now represented more than their own self-interest; they also represented the university. Thus, agency was enlarged as they became both individual and representative agents.

President Henry D. Moyle, a counselor to President David O. McKay, explained the principle of agency in a complementary manner in a missionary meeting many years ago.

"Apparently [President Moyle] had been told that some missionaries in the mission had said that they had their 'free agency' and therefore didn't have to get up at six in the morning unless they wanted to. President Moyle explained that it had been [their] right to choose whether [they] served a mission or not, but now, having chosen to serve a mission, [they] had exhausted [their] agency on that matter. [The missionaries] now had no right but to get up in the morning and do the other things required of a good missionary" (Joseph Fielding McConkie, *Understanding the Power God Gives Us,* 22).

Therefore, exercising and "exhausting" or expending our agency is (1) to act as agents by (2) electing to live in accordance with revealed truth and (3) binding ourselves to the blessings, ongoing obligations, and consequences associated with that action. The pattern of making, remembering, and honoring sacred covenants is then, in essence, a freewill, voluntary return of our agency to God. Ultimately, the only gift we can ever give to the Lord is our moral agency. Each successive use of our agency to come under covenant is a mortal and submissive vow of "nevertheless not my will, but thine, be done" (Luke 22:42). Each covenant condition is a step in the ongoing process of turning away from selfishness and to the Lord, of coming unto Christ, of being perfected in him, and of denying ourselves of all ungodliness (see Moroni 10:32).

President Boyd K. Packer poignantly described one of the great lessons of his life—a lesson about giving his agency to God.

"Perhaps the greatest discovery of my life, without question the greatest commitment, came when finally I had the confidence in God that I would loan or yield my agency to Him—without compulsion or pressure, without any duress, as a single individual alone, by myself, no counterfeiting, nothing expected other than the privilege. In a sense, speaking figuratively, to take one's agency, that precious gift which the scriptures make plain is essential to life itself, and say, 'I will do as thou directs,' is afterward to learn that in so doing you possess it all the more" (*That All May Be Edified*, 256–57).

President Packer's teaching that agency is expanded as we yield to God's will certainly contradicts the prevalent philosophies and patterns of the world. Many secular voices declare that obedience to the commandments of God is restricting and stifling. However, precisely the opposite is true. The unrighteous exercise of agency shackles us with the consequences of our constraining choices. Obedience, on the other hand, is liberating and enlivening. Moral agency expands endlessly when exercised righteously. Acting in doctrine yields the ever-increasing blessings of assurance, direction, protection, and joy.

It can take a tremendous amount of faith and courage to recognize and accept the will of God in our lives. Several years ago there was a young father who had been active in the Church as a boy but had chosen a different path during his teenage years. After serving in the military, he married a lovely girl, and soon children blessed their home.

One day without warning their little four-year-old daughter became critically ill and was hospitalized. In desperation and for the first time in many years, the father was found on his knees in prayer, asking that the life of his daughter be spared. Yet her condition worsened. Gradually, this father sensed that his little girl would not live, and slowly his prayers changed; he no longer prayed for healing but rather for understanding. "Let Thy will be done" was now the manner of his pleadings.

Soon his daughter was in a coma, and the father knew her hours on earth were few. Fortified with understanding, trust, and power beyond their own, the young parents prayed again, asking for the opportunity to hold her close once more while she was awake. The daughter's eyes opened, and her frail arms reached out to her parents for one final embrace. And then she was gone. This father knew their prayers had been answered—a kind, compassionate Father in Heaven had comforted their hearts. God's will had been done, and they had gained understanding (adapted from H. Burke Peterson, "Adversity and Prayer," 18).

One of the most well-known and frequently cited passages of scripture is Moses 1:39. This verse clearly and concisely describes the work of the Eternal Father: "For behold, this is my work and my glory—to bring to pass the immortality and eternal life of man."

A companion scripture found in the Doctrine and Covenants describes with equal clarity and conciseness our primary work as the sons and daughters of the Eternal Father. Interestingly, this verse does not seem to be as well-known and is not quoted with great frequency. "Behold, this is your work, to keep my commandments, yea, with all your might, mind and strength" (Doctrine and Covenants 11:20).

Thus, the Father's work is to bring to pass the immortality and eternal life of His children. Our work is to keep His commandments with all of our might, mind, and strength. Our agency is to be used to act in His doctrine.

See DVD Segment 16

Conditions of the Baptismal Covenant

The covenant associated with the ordinance of baptism provides a strong example of the relationship between covenants and moral agency. The fundamental conditions of the covenant we agree to as we enter the waters of baptism are these: we witness that we are willing to take upon ourselves the name of Jesus Christ, that we will always remember Him, and that we will keep His commandments. The promised blessing for honoring this covenant is that we may always have His Spirit to be with us (see Doctrine and Covenants 20:77).

We can learn much from the sequence of these covenant conditions. First, we pledge our willingness to take upon ourselves the name of Jesus Christ (see Alma 46:15). Spiritual rebirth and a mighty change of heart (see Mosiah 5:2; Alma 5:12–14) are commenced as we turn to the Lord and away from selfishness and are cleansed from sin by proper baptism. We pledge to "come unto Christ" (Omni 1:26) and "deny [ourselves] of all ungodliness" (Moroni 10:32). And we commit to represent Him and bear His name appropriately "at all times and in all things, and in all places that [we] may be in, even until death" (Mosiah 18:9). Individuals baptized and confirmed as members of The Church of Jesus Christ of Latter-day Saints exercise their agency to move beyond their self-interest, to turn outward, and to become representatives of the Lord.

As "representative agents," we have a responsibility to live in such a way that our example represents well the Savior whose name we have pledged our willingness to take upon us. The power of setting a righteous example came into greater focus for me in 1980, when Sister Bednar and I and our sons moved to Arkansas after I had completed my studies at Purdue University. Susan and I were excited to learn if life truly existed after graduate school. We anticipated with great excitement the adventure of a new start for our family in a wonderful community.

One of our sons had a challenging learning experience at his elementary school one day as several children told him they could not play with him during recess because he was a Mormon and not a Christian. This little boy came home after school and asked why the other children had said such things and acted as they did. We simply told him that they did not know much about our beliefs and Church—and that he would have a terrific opportunity to be a missionary.

In the months and many years that followed, this son and his two brothers, along with a small number of other faithful Latter-day Saint youth who lived in the area, endeavored to be good examples as they participated in a wide range of school activities, countless athletic contests, and many community events. Our sons certainly were not perfect; they were quite normal, fun-loving, and typically rambunctious boys. But our boys did strive to live the gospel and to be examples of the believers "in word, in conversation, in charity, in spirit, in faith, in purity" (1 Timothy 4:12). They declined invitations to play on all-star athletic teams if Sunday practices and play were expected. And they did not participate in activities or events that would compromise their standards.

As these three young men progressed through both junior high and high school, Susan and I were intrigued to learn that the parents of our sons' friends frequently would ask their children if the Bednar boys were going to attend a party or some other activity. Interestingly, if the answer were yes, then those parents would permit their children to attend. If the answer were no, then many parents often would not allow their children to participate. Oh how we continue to cherish the associations and friendships we developed with the parents of our sons' friends—good and God-fearing men and women who were not members of our Church.

In 1997 we moved from Arkansas to Rexburg, Idaho, so I could assume my new responsibilities as president of Ricks College, now Brigham Young University–Idaho. As we were preparing to relocate, I called upon and talked with a number of friends with whom we had associated for many years. I asked a favor of one good friend to whom I previously had given a copy of the Book of Mormon and with whom I had often talked about the Savior's restored Church. I indicated to my friend that falsehoods about our Church and our beliefs often were promulgated in our community. He readily acknowledged that such things occurred. I then asked for his help. He responded that he would gladly be of assistance. I gave him a copy of Elder M. Russell Ballard's book *Our Search for Happiness: An Invitation to Understand The Church of Jesus Christ of Latter-day Saints* and requested that he read it. I explained to him that since I would no longer be in a position to explain our beliefs and defend our Church, I needed him to do so. I invited him to become a defender of our faith in a community where Latter-day Saints often were maligned and mocked.

He scanned the table of contents of the book I had given him, he paused for a moment, and then he said sincerely, "Dave, I will." And then he added, "We have been watching the LDS kids in the schools over the years, and we all know that you Latter-day Saints have something we do not have. I will do my best to help stop the falsehoods."

Such a dramatic change of perspective in just a few short years—from an elementary school playground and the taunting of a little LDS boy because he allegedly was not a Christian to an acknowledgment by prominent parents in the community that "you Latter-day Saints have something we do not have." By exercising their moral agency to represent the Lord faithfully, those young people extended the reach of their influence to the point that even a person not of our faith would essentially become an agent in defending the values of the Church. Such is the power of moral agency and devoted discipleship.

Elder Dallin H. Oaks has explained that in renewing our baptismal covenants by partaking of the emblems of the sacrament, "we do not witness that we *take upon us* the name of Jesus Christ. [Rather, we] witness that we are *willing* to do so. (See D&C 20:77.) The fact that we only witness to our willingness suggests that something else must happen before we actually take that sacred name upon us in the [ultimate and] most important sense" ("Taking upon Us the Name of Jesus Christ," 81). The baptismal covenant clearly contemplates a future event or events and looks forward to the temple.

In modern revelations the Lord refers to temples as houses "built unto my name" (Doctrine and Covenants 105:33; see also 109:2–5; 124:39). In the dedicatory prayer of the Kirtland Temple, the Prophet Joseph Smith petitioned the Father "that thy servants may go forth from this house armed with thy power, and that thy name may be upon them" (Doctrine and Covenants 109:22). He also asked for a blessing "over thy people upon whom thy name shall be put in this house" (v. 26). And as the Lord appeared in and accepted the Kirtland Temple as His house, He declared, "For behold, I have accepted this house, and my name shall be here; and I will manifest myself to my people in mercy in this house" (Doctrine and Covenants 110:7).

These scriptures help us understand that the process of taking upon ourselves the name of Jesus Christ that is commenced in the waters of baptism is continued and enlarged in the house of the Lord. As we stand in the waters of baptism, we look to the temple. As we partake of the sacrament, we look to the temple. We pledge to always remember the Savior and to keep His commandments as preparation to participate in the sacred ordinances of the temple and receive the highest blessings available through the name and by the authority of the Lord Jesus Christ. Thus, in the ordinances of the holy temple we more completely and fully take upon us the name of Jesus Christ and become better qualified to represent Him.

For those individuals who have received and are striving to honor baptismal and temple covenants, the third commandment suggests a particularly pointed implication: "Thou shalt not take the name of the Lord thy God in vain: for the Lord will not hold him guiltless that taketh his name in vain" (Deuteronomy 5:11).

This commandment focuses upon much more than the use of inappropriate language. When we knowingly violate covenant conditions after having pledged our willingness to take upon ourselves the name of Jesus Christ, we literally are taking His name in vain.

The second basic element of the baptismal covenant is that we will always remember Him.

"Some trust in chariots, and some in horses: but we will *remember* the name of the Lord our God" (Psalm 20:7; emphasis added).

"O *remember, remember,* my sons, the words which king Benjamin spake unto his people; yea, *remember* that there is no other way nor means whereby man can be saved, only through the atoning blood of Jesus Christ, who shall come; yea, *remember* that he cometh to redeem the world" (Helaman 5:9; emphasis added).

"And behold, when I see many of my brethren truly penitent, and coming to the Lord their God, then is my soul filled with joy; then do I *remember* what the Lord has done for me, yea, even that he hath heard my prayer; yea, then do I *remember* his merciful arm which he extended towards me" (Alma 29:10; emphasis added).

"And I would exhort you, my beloved brethren, that ye *remember* that every good gift cometh of Christ" (Moroni 10:18; emphasis added).

"Behold, my beloved brethren, *remember* the words of your God; pray unto him continually by day, and give thanks unto his holy name by night. Let your hearts rejoice" (2 Nephi 9:52; emphasis added).

"And I, Nephi, have written these things unto my people, that perhaps I might persuade them that they would *remember* the Lord their Redeemer" (1 Nephi 19:18; emphasis added).

Studying, pondering, and feasting upon the words of Christ (see 2 Nephi 31:20) as recorded in the holy scriptures will help us to always remember Him. Praying continually (see Alma 62:51; Alma 13:28; Moroni 8:3) helps us to always remember Him. And faithfully acting in His doctrine helps us to always remember Him. Thus, a willingness to take upon ourselves the Savior's name and to effectively represent Him is related directly to always remembering

Him—His character, perfections, and attributes; His mortal mission; His gospel; His commandments; and His promised blessings.

The third basic element of the baptismal covenant is that we will keep His commandments.

"Now I say unto you, if this be the desire of your hearts, what have you against being baptized in the name of the Lord, as a witness before him that ye have entered into a covenant with him, that ye will serve him and keep his commandments, that he may pour out his Spirit more abundantly upon you?" (Mosiah 18:10).

In counseling with members of the Church, I have listened to individuals justify sinful behavior with the statement, "Well, I have my agency and can choose not to keep the commandments." Such a comment reveals a serious lack of knowledge about and understanding of the principle of moral agency.

Indeed, we may choose not to honor our sacred obligations. But such action is not simply another individual episode of exercising agency; rather, it is violating or breaking a covenant with God, turning away from and failing to remember Him, and repudiating His name and our responsibility to represent Him. Disobedience is rejection of and rebellion against the terms and conditions specified by God for our progress and happiness.

"Behold, the Lord requireth the heart and a willing mind; and the willing and obedient shall eat the good of the land of Zion in these last days.

"And the rebellious shall be cut off out of the land of Zion, and shall be sent away, and shall not inherit the land.

"For, verily I say that the rebellious are not of the blood of Ephraim, wherefore they shall be plucked out" (Doctrine and Covenants 64:34–36).

Our mortal journey is marked by progressive covenants that invite us to exercise our moral agency in righteousness—to choose

God and to love our brothers and sisters (see Moses 7:33). The baptismal covenant is the first in a succession of gospel covenants that enable us to turn from self to the Savior. Once we have used our agency to pledge our willingness to take upon ourselves the Savior's name, to accept the covenant responsibilities of remembering and representing Him, and to bind ourselves to act in all holiness, disobedience brings more serious and spiritually devastating consequences.

We offend God.

"And in nothing doth man offend God, or against none is his wrath kindled, save those who confess not his hand in all things, and obey not his commandments" (Doctrine and Covenants 59:21).

We turn away from the light and life of the world (see 3 Nephi 11:11) and toward the darkness.

See DVD Segment 10

"Then spake Jesus again unto them, saying, I am the light of the world: he that followeth me shall not walk in darkness, but shall have the light of life" (John 8:12).

We "withdraw [ourselves] from the Spirit of the Lord, that it may have no place in [us] to guide [us] in wisdom's paths that [we] may be blessed, prospered, and preserved" (Mosiah 2:36).

We cease to "press forward with a steadfastness in Christ" (2 Nephi 31:20) and regress. We "put off" the progress we may have made in becoming a saint through the Atonement of Christ the Lord and put back on "the natural man [which] is an enemy to God" (Mosiah 3:19).

We block or halt altogether our access to the ordinances of the holy temple that enable us to more completely take upon ourselves the name of Jesus Christ and more faithfully represent Him.

We are cut off.

"Hearken, O ye people who *profess my name,* saith the Lord

your God; for behold, mine anger is kindled against the rebellious, and they shall know mine arm and mine indignation, in the day of visitation and of wrath upon the nations.

"And he that will not take up his cross and follow me, and keep my commandments, the same shall not be saved.

"Behold, I, the Lord, command; and he that will not obey shall be *cut off* in mine own due time, after I have commanded and the commandment is broken" (Doctrine and Covenants 56:1–3; emphasis added).

Truly, "of him unto whom much is given much is required; and he who sins against the greater light shall receive the greater condemnation" (Doctrine and Covenants 82:3).

During the years I served as a stake president, I had many opportunities to visit in the homes of less-active members of the Church, people I would describe as having turned away from the light. I often would contact one of the bishops and invite him to prayerfully identify individuals or families we could visit together. Before traveling to a home, the bishop and I would kneel and petition our Heavenly Father for guidance and inspiration, for us and for the members with whom we would meet.

Our visits were quite straightforward. We expressed love and appreciation for the opportunity to be in their home. We affirmed that we were servants of the Lord on His errand to their home. We indicated that we missed and needed them—and that they needed the blessings of the restored gospel. And at some point early in our conversation I often would ask a question like this: "Will you please help us understand why you are not actively participating in the blessings and programs of the Church?"

I made hundreds and hundreds of such visits. Each individual, each family, each home, and each answer was different. Over the years, however, I detected a common theme in many of the answers to my questions. Frequently responses like these were given:

"Several years ago a man said something in Sunday School that offended me, and I have not been back since."

"No one in this branch greeted or reached out to me. I felt like an outsider. I was hurt by the unfriendliness of this branch."

"I did not agree with the counsel the bishop gave me. I will not step foot in that building again as long as he is serving in that position."

Many other causes of offense were cited—from doctrinal differences among adults to taunting, teasing, and excluding by youth. But the recurring theme was: "I was offended by . . ."

The bishop and I would listen intently and sincerely. One of us might next ask about their conversion to and testimony of the restored gospel. As we talked, eyes often were moist with tears as these good people recalled the confirming witness of the Holy Ghost and described their prior spiritual experiences. Most of the "less-active" people I have ever visited had a discernible and tender testimony of the truthfulness of the restored gospel. However, they were not presently participating in Church activities and meetings.

And then I would say something like this. "Let me make sure I understand what has happened to you. Because someone at church offended you, you have not been blessed by the ordinance of the sacrament. You have withdrawn yourself from the constant companionship of the Holy Ghost. Because someone at church offended you, you have cut yourself off from priesthood ordinances and the holy temple. You have discontinued your opportunity to serve others and to learn and grow. And you are leaving barriers that will impede the spiritual progress of your children, your children's children, and the generations that will follow." Many times people would think for a moment and then respond: "I have never thought about it that way."

The bishop and I would then extend an invitation: "Dear friend, we are here today to counsel you that the time to stop being offended is now. Not only do we need you, but you need the blessings of the restored gospel of Jesus Christ. Please come back—now."

When we believe or say we have been offended, we usually mean we feel insulted, mistreated, snubbed, or disrespected. And certainly clumsy, embarrassing, unprincipled, and mean-spirited things do occur in our interactions with other people that would allow us to take offense. However, it ultimately is impossible for another person to offend you or to offend me. Indeed, believing that another person offended us is fundamentally false. To be offended is a *choice* we make; it is not a *condition* inflicted or imposed upon us by someone or something else.

To believe that someone or something can *make* us feel offended, angry, hurt, or bitter diminishes our moral agency and transforms us into objects to be acted upon. As agents, however, you and I have the power to act and to choose how we will respond to an offensive or hurtful situation. We cannot control the intentions or behavior of other people. However, we do determine how we will act. Please remember that you and I are agents endowed with moral agency, and we can choose not to be offended.

During a perilous period of war, an exchange of letters occurred between Moroni, the captain of the Nephite armies, and Pahoran, the chief judge and governor of the land. Moroni, whose army was suffering because of inadequate support from the government, wrote to Pahoran "by the way of condemnation" (Alma 60:2) and harshly accused him of thoughtlessness, slothfulness, and neglect. Pahoran might easily have resented Moroni and his message, but he chose not to take offense. Pahoran responded compassionately and described a rebellion against the government about which Moroni was not aware. And then he responded, "Behold, I say unto you, Moroni, that I do not joy in your great afflictions, yea, it grieves my soul. . . . And now, in your epistle you have censured me, but it mattereth not; I am not angry, but do rejoice in the greatness of your heart" (Alma 61:2, 9).

One of the greatest indicators of our own spiritual maturity is revealed in how we respond to the weaknesses, the inexperience, and the potentially offensive actions of others. A thing, an event, or an expression may be offensive, but you and I can choose not to be offended—and to say with Pahoran, "it mattereth not."

As with the choice to be offended, all our choices have consequences. When we choose to act as agents in righteous ways, the correctness of our decisions is ratified by the Spirit. Faithfully obeying God's commandments is essential to our receiving the Holy Ghost. We are reminded of this truth each week as we listen to the sacrament prayers and worthily partake of the bread and water. As we pledge our willingness to take upon ourselves the name of Jesus Christ, to always remember Him, and to keep His commandments, we are promised that we may always have His Spirit to be with us (see Doctrine and Covenants 20:77). And the companionship of and assistance we receive from the Holy Ghost are essential if we are to appropriately fulfill our responsibility to represent Him at all times and in all places.

Continue as You Commenced

The word *commence* in its various forms is used seventy-three times in the scriptures. To commence denotes beginning, entering upon, and initiating formally by taking a first step.

For example, the numberless concourses of people in Lehi's vision of the tree of life are described as *"commenc[ing]* in the path which led to the tree" (1 Nephi 8:22; emphasis added).

Alma expressed his joy to his son Shiblon:

"And now, my son, I trust that I shall have great joy in you, because of your steadiness and your faithfulness unto God; for as you have *commenced* in your youth to look to the Lord your God, even so I hope that you will continue in keeping his commandments; for blessed is he that endureth to the end" (Alma 38:2; emphasis added).

In both of these scriptures, commencing is clearly about beginnings. But I believe the scriptures teach us that true commencing is much more than simply starting or initiating; it also suggests a responsibility to sustain and endure "valiantly" (Doctrine and Covenants 121:29) in that which is right and good and praiseworthy. Thus, Alma admonished his son to "continue in keeping his commandments."

See DVD Segment 18

Oliver Cowdery, who acted as the Prophet Joseph Smith's principal scribe during the translation of the Book of Mormon, learned a valuable lesson about the importance of commencing and continuing. Oliver desired to have the gift of translation and was instructed by the Lord:

"And, behold, I grant unto you a gift, if you desire of me, to translate, even as my servant Joseph. . . .

"And now I command you, that if you have good desires—a desire to lay up treasures for yourself in heaven—then shall you assist in bringing to light, with your gift, those parts of my scriptures which have been hidden because of iniquity.

"And now, behold, I give unto you, and also unto my servant Joseph, the keys of this gift, which shall bring to light this ministry;

and in the mouth of two or three witnesses shall every word be established" (Doctrine and Covenants 6:25, 27–28).

Apparently Oliver delayed or postponed the exercise of the spiritual gift he had received. Therefore, in a subsequent revelation given to Oliver Cowdery through Joseph Smith the Prophet, Oliver was admonished concerning his role in the work of translation.

"Be patient, my son, for it is wisdom in me, and it is not expedient that you should translate at this present time.

"Behold, the work which you are called to do is to write for my servant Joseph.

"And, behold, it is because that you did not *continue as you commenced,* when you began to translate, that I have taken away this privilege from you.

"Do not murmur, my son, for it is wisdom in me that I have dealt with you after this manner" (Doctrine and Covenants 9:3–6; emphasis added).

Consider the penetrating phrase, "you did not continue as you commenced." The righteous exercise of moral agency to accept covenant responsibilities and promised blessings requires each of us to both commence and continue. Commencing is necessary but not sufficient. Commencing also requires sustained acting in doctrine and faithfully pressing forward. The obligations are great and may sometimes seem overwhelming. But through the "merits, and mercy, and grace of the Holy Messiah" (2 Nephi 2:8) we can be blessed and strengthened to do what the Lord wants us to do so we can become what He intends for us to become.

Two passages of scripture summarize the importance of continuing as we have commenced.

"And Jesus said unto him, No man, having put his hand to the plough, and looking back, is fit for the kingdom of God" (Luke 9:62).

"Wherefore, ye must press forward with a steadfastness in Christ, having a perfect brightness of hope, and a love of God and of all men. Wherefore, if ye shall press forward, feasting upon the word of Christ, and endure to the end, behold, thus saith the Father: Ye shall have eternal life" (2 Nephi 31:20).

Summary

Many times the disparity between what we know about the doctrines and principles of the Savior's restored gospel and how we live is caused by incomplete or inaccurate knowledge. A correct understanding of the Father's plan of happiness, of the Atonement, of moral agency, and of covenants is essential for every member of The Church of Jesus Christ of Latter-day Saints. As we increase in learning about these basic truths, our capacity to act in doctrine is enlarged, extended, and strengthened. We are blessed with eyes to see that obedience is the sweet fruit of honoring covenant responsibilities—not merely a chore or an option to be performed based upon circumstances or convenience. We more fully recognize the importance of pledging our willingness to take upon ourselves the name of Jesus Christ. And we gain an appreciation for both the individual and the representative aspects of moral agency.

A familiar hymn is entitled "Choose the Right" for a reason. We have not been blessed with agency to choose whatever we want whenever we will. Rather, moral agency enables us as agents to turn from self to the Savior, to pledge our willingness to take His name upon us, to love one another and choose God, and to bind ourselves to faithfully act in His doctrine.

RELATED READINGS FOR CHAPTER TWO

The two related readings for Chapter Two emphasize the truth that you and I are agents with the power and capacity to act; we are not objects to be acted upon. Agency is the source of our capacity to act in doctrine.

"And Nothing Shall Offend Them"
Ensign, November 2006, 89–92

To be offended is a choice we make; it is not a condition inflicted or imposed upon us by someone or something else. Through the strengthening power of the Atonement, you and I can be blessed to avoid and triumph over offense by turning from self and to the Savior.

"Honorably Hold a Name and Standing"
Ensign, May 2009, 97–100

Agency is exercised and expressed most completely as we accept the conditions of gospel covenants as established by God. We are guided and protected as we honor sacred covenant obligations and press forward with faith in the Savior.

CONSIDER

What can and should I do to gain more knowledge about and increase my understanding of the role of moral agency in the Father's plan?

Consider

What am I learning about moral agency that can help me as I work to reduce the disparity between what I know and what I do?

CONSIDER

As I continue to turn from self to the Savior, what can and should I do to more fully remember and honor my covenants?

My Own Questions to Consider

Scriptures Related to What I Am Learning

Scriptures Related to What I Am Learning

AN INVITATION TO LEARN AND ACT

What additional doctrines and principles, if understood, would help me increasingly to become an agent who acts and not an object that is acted upon?	What can and should I do to "act in" those doctrines and principles?	How will I know if I am making progress in becoming an anxiously engaged agent?

AN INVITATION TO LEARN AND ACT

What additional doctrines and principles, if understood, would help me increasingly to become an agent who acts and not an object that is acted upon?	What can and should I do to "act in" those doctrines and principles?	How will I know if I am making progress in becoming an anxiously engaged agent?

AN INVITATION TO LEARN AND ACT		
What additional doctrines and principles, if understood, would help me increasingly to become an agent who acts and not an object that is acted upon?	What can and should I do to "act in" those doctrines and principles?	How will I know if I am making progress in becoming an anxiously engaged agent?

CHAPTER THREE

ACTING IN DOCTRINE AND CONVERSION UNTO THE LORD

As we increase in learning, turn to the Savior, and act in doctrine, our personal testimonies of Him and of His gospel are strengthened and we become more fully converted.

In our homes and Church meetings, we often teach and talk about testimonies. We define what a testimony is, we learn how a testimony is gained and nurtured, and we identify ways whereby a testimony can be strengthened. We also often teach and talk about conversion. We describe the steps in the conversion process, we review the many blessings that come into our lives as we more completely "come unto Christ" (Moroni 10:32) and become converted, and we consider ways we can help other individuals and families press forward on the pathway of conversion to Christ. Typically, however, we treat these two essential topics separately and independently. We gain both precious perspective and greater conviction as we consider the essential connection between personal testimony and ongoing conversion.

TESTIMONY

Testimony is personal knowledge, based upon the confirming witness of the Holy Ghost, that certain facts of eternal significance are true. The Holy Ghost, even the third member of the Godhead, is the messenger for the Father and the Son; He also is the teacher of and guide to all truth (see John 14:26; 16:13). Thus, "by the power of the Holy Ghost [we] may know the truth of all things" (Moroni 10:5).

The knowledge and spiritual conviction we receive from the Holy Ghost are the result of revelation. Seeking for and obtaining these blessings require a sincere heart, real intent, and faith in the Lord Jesus Christ (see Moroni 10:4). And such a personal testimony also brings responsibility, duty, and accountability.

Please consider the power and simplicity of the following three scriptural examples of personal testimony.

Long ago Job declared publicly what he had learned privately in his heart.

"For I know that my redeemer liveth, and that he shall stand at the latter day upon the earth: And though after my skin worms destroy this body, yet in my flesh shall I see God" (Job 19:25–26).

The Apostle Peter likewise proclaimed his spiritual witness of the Savior.

"When Jesus came into the coasts of Caesarea Philippi, he asked his disciples, saying, Whom do men say that I the Son of man am?

"And they said, Some say that thou art John the Baptist: some, Elias; and others, Jeremias, or one of the prophets.

"He saith unto them, But whom say ye that I am?

"And Simon Peter answered and said, Thou art the Christ, the Son of the living God.

"And Jesus answered and said unto him, Blessed art thou, Simon Bar-jona: for flesh and blood hath not revealed it unto thee, but my Father which is in heaven" (Matthew 16:13–17).

Alma bore strong witness of the Savior throughout his ministry.

"And this is not all. Do ye not suppose that I know of these things myself? Behold, I testify unto you that I do know that these things whereof I have spoken are true. And how do ye suppose that I know of their surety?

"Behold, I say unto you they are made known unto me by the Holy Spirit of God. Behold, I have fasted and prayed many days that I might know these things of myself. And now I do know of myself that they are true; for the Lord God hath made them manifest unto me by his Holy Spirit; and this is the spirit of revelation which is in me.

"And moreover, I say unto you that it has thus been revealed unto me, that the words which have been spoken by our fathers are true, even so according to the spirit of prophecy which is in me, which is also by the manifestation of the Spirit of God.

"I say unto you, that I know of myself that whatsoever I shall say unto you, concerning that which is to come, is true; and I say unto you, that I know that Jesus Christ shall come, yea, the Son, the Only Begotten of the Father, full of grace, and mercy, and truth. And behold, it is he that cometh to take away the sins of the world, yea, the sins of every man who steadfastly believeth on his name" (Alma 5:45–48).

As these examples illustrate, a testimony is personal knowledge of spiritual truth. A testimony is the result of the Holy Ghost confirming the reality of truth to our souls (see Moroni 10:4–5).

Knowing that Heavenly Father lives and loves us, that Jesus Christ is our Redeemer and Savior, and that the gospel of Jesus Christ is true and has been restored to the earth in its fullness in the latter days are fundamental components of a testimony.

TESTIMONY AND CONVERSION

Conversion is described in the scriptures as putting off the natural man (see Mosiah 3:19), experiencing a mighty change of heart (see Alma 5:12–14), undergoing a spiritual rebirth (see Mosiah 27:24–25), and becoming a new creature in Christ (see 2 Corinthians 5:17). Please note that the conversion described in these verses is mighty, not minor—a spiritual rebirth and fundamental change of what we think and feel, what we desire and do, and what we are and strive to become. Indeed, the essence of the gospel of Jesus Christ entails a fundamental and permanent change in our very nature made possible through the Atonement of the Savior. As we turn to and follow the Master, we choose to change our hearts—to be spiritually reborn.

As Alma declared:

"Marvel not that all mankind, yea, men and women, all nations, kindreds, tongues and people, must be born again; yea, born of God, changed from their carnal and fallen state, to a state of righteousness, being redeemed of God, becoming his sons and daughters;

"And thus they become new creatures; and unless they do this, they can in nowise inherit the kingdom of God" (Mosiah 27:25–26).

True conversion brings a change in one's beliefs, heart, and life to accept and conform to the will of God and includes a conscious commitment to become a disciple of Christ and to act in His doctrine.

The Book of Mormon is filled with inspiring descriptions of continuing and deepening conversion. Amaleki, a descendant of Jacob charged with keeping the sacred record, was born in the days of Mosiah and learned gospel principles from King Benjamin. He declared, "And now, my beloved brethren, I would that ye should come unto Christ, who is the Holy One of Israel, and partake of his salvation, and the power of his redemption. Yea, come unto him, and offer your whole souls as an offering unto him" (Omni 1:26).

Knowing by the power of the Holy Ghost that Jesus is the Christ is a good, an important, and a necessary thing. But earnestly coming unto Him and giving our whole souls as an offering requires much more than merely knowing. Continuing conversion requires all of our heart, all of our mind, and all of our might and strength (see Doctrine and Covenants 4:2). Two additional examples from the Book of Mormon illustrate this truth.

King Benjamin's people responded to his teaching by exclaiming with one voice: "Yea, we believe all the words which thou hast spoken unto us; and also, we know of their surety and truth, because of the Spirit of the Lord Omnipotent, which has wrought a mighty change in us, or in our hearts, that we have no more disposition to do evil, but to do good continually" (Mosiah 5:2).

Accepting the words that had been spoken and gaining a testimony of their surety and truth produced a mighty change of heart—and a firm commitment to improve, to act in doctrine, and to become better.

The converted Lamanites who lived at the time of Samuel the Lamanite are described as "in the path of their duty, and they do walk circumspectly before God, and they do observe to keep his commandments and his statutes and his judgments . . . the more part of them are doing this, and they are striving with unwearied diligence that they may bring the remainder of their brethren to the knowledge of the truth" (Helaman 15:5–6).

Note from these examples the key characteristics associated with conversion: experiencing a mighty change in our hearts, having no more disposition to do evil but to do good continually, going forward in the path of duty, walking circumspectly before God, observing to keep the commandments, striving and serving with unwearied diligence. Clearly, the testimonies and spiritual development of these faithful souls produced the fruit of steadfast devotion to the Lord and His teachings.

For most of us, conversion does not occur quickly or all at once; it is an ongoing process and not a one-time event that results from a dramatic or overpowering experience. Line upon line and precept upon precept, gradually and almost imperceptibly, our motives, our thoughts, our words, and our deeds become aligned with the will of God. Continuing conversion unto the Lord requires both persistence and patience.

If you and I sincerely desire to become converted unto the Lord, we must build appropriately and effectively upon Him as our foundation.

"And now, my sons, remember, remember that it is upon the rock of our Redeemer, who is Christ, the Son of God, that ye must build your foundation; that when the devil shall send forth his mighty winds, yea, his shafts in the whirlwind, yea, when all his hail and his mighty storm shall beat upon you, it shall have no power over you to drag you down to the gulf of misery and endless wo, because of the rock upon which ye are built, which is a sure foundation, a foundation whereon if men build they cannot fall" (Helaman 5:12).

As this verse affirms, the Lord Jesus Christ is a sure foundation. And you and I cannot and will not falter spiritually if we establish our lives upon Him and His gospel. This is a truly remarkable and faith-promoting promise.

The pattern we must follow to become more deeply converted unto the Lord is outlined simply and clearly in Helaman 15:7–8.

"And behold, ye do know of yourselves, for ye have witnessed it, that as many of them as are brought to the knowledge of the truth, and to know of the wicked and abominable traditions of their fathers, and are led to believe the holy scriptures, yea, the prophecies of the holy prophets, which are written, which leadeth them to faith on the Lord, and unto repentance, which faith and repentance bringeth a change of heart unto them—

"Therefore, as many as have come to this, ye know of yourselves are firm and steadfast in the faith, and in the thing wherewith they have been made free."

Please notice the specific steps identified in these verses: (1) belief in the teachings and prophecies of the holy prophets as recorded in the scriptures fosters (2) faith in the Lord Jesus Christ. Faith in the Savior leads to (3) repentance. Faith in Christ and repentance bring about (4) the mighty change of heart. Therefore, as many as have diligently and faithfully followed these steps are (5) firm and steadfast in the faith. This is the pathway of conversion unto the Lord.

See DVD Segment 2

A testimony is the beginning of and a prerequisite to conversion unto the Lord. A testimony is a point of departure; it is not an ultimate destination. A strong testimony is the necessary foundation upon which conversion is established. A testimony is the initial step on the pathway of ongoing and deepening conversion.

A testimony alone is not and will not be enough to protect us in the latter-day storm of evil and religious persecution in which we do now and will yet live. A testimony is both important and necessary, but it is not sufficient to provide the spiritual strength and protection we need. Some members of the Church with testimonies have wavered and fallen away. Their spiritual witness and resolve did not measure up to the challenges they encountered. Testimony must lead to ongoing and deepening conversion to the Lord Jesus Christ.

Every member of The Church of Jesus Christ of Latter-day Saints who has been baptized by proper authority and received the gift of the Holy Ghost by the laying on of hands has some measure of testimony. However, not every member of the Church is necessarily converted unto the Lord. Recall the Savior's admonition to Peter:

"And the Lord said, Simon, Simon, behold, Satan hath desired to have you, that he may sift you as wheat:

"But I have prayed for thee, that thy faith fail not: and *when thou art converted,* strengthen thy brethren" (Luke 22:31–32; emphasis added).

This mighty Apostle had served with the Lord throughout most of His mortal ministry and participated in and witnessed many miracles. Yet even Peter needed additional instruction about the converting power of the Holy Ghost and the obligation to serve faithfully and diligently.

An important lesson about the connection between personal testimony and ongoing conversion is evident in the missionary labors of the sons of Mosiah. These faithful and diligent missionaries were blessed with much success among the Lamanites.

"And thousands were brought to the knowledge of the Lord . . .

"And as sure as the Lord liveth, so sure as many as believed, or as many as were brought to the knowledge of the truth, through the preaching of Ammon and his brethren, according to the spirit of revelation and of prophecy, and the power of God working miracles in them—yea, I say unto you, as the Lord liveth, as many of the Lamanites as believed in their preaching, and were converted unto the Lord, never did fall away.

"For they became a righteous people; they did lay down the weapons of their rebellion, that they did not fight against God any more, neither against any of their brethren.

"Now, these are they who were converted unto the Lord" (Alma 23:5–8).

Notice that as many of the Lamanites as were brought to the knowledge of the truth and converted unto the Lord *never did fall away!* The two major elements described in these verses are (1) *the knowledge of the truth,* which may be considered a testimony, and (2) *converted unto the Lord,* which I understand to be ongoing conversion to the Savior and His gospel. Thus, the powerful combination of both personal testimony and conversion unto the Lord produced firmness and steadfastness and provided spiritual protection. These faithful disciples never did fall away, and they did lay down the weapons of their rebellion.

To lay down cherished "weapons of rebellion" requires more than merely believing and knowing. Conviction, commitment, repentance, and submissiveness precede the discarding of our weapons of rebellion. Do you and I still possess weapons of rebellion that keep us from becoming more fully converted unto the Lord? If so, then we need to surrender and repent—and we need to do so now.

Also note that the Lamanites were not converted to the missionaries who taught them. They were not converted to the excellent programs provided by the Church. They were not converted to the personalities of the leaders who served them. They were not converted to preserving a cultural heritage or the traditions of their fathers. They were converted unto the Lord—to Him as the Savior, to His Atonement, to His doctrine, to His covenants and ordinances, to His commandments—and they never did fall away. Thus, a testimony that develops and grows into conversion yields greater consistency in living that which we know and understand is true. This truth applies in precisely the same manner to you and to me today.

Elder Marion G. Romney highlighted the central role of the Savior and of His Atonement in the relationship between testimony and conversion:

"A testimony comes when the Holy Ghost gives the earnest seeker a witness of the truth. A moving testimony vitalizes faith; that is, it induces repentance and obedience to the commandments. Conversion, on the other hand, is the fruit of, or the reward for, repentance and obedience. Conversion is effected by divine forgiveness, which remits sins. Thus [the earnest seeker] is converted to a newness of life. His spirit is healed" (in Conference Report, October 1963, 24).

See DVD Segment 1

Whereas a testimony is spiritual knowledge of truth obtained through the power of the Holy Ghost, conversion is deepening devotion to and consistent application of the knowledge we have received. Knowing that the gospel is true is the essence of testimony. Consistently being true to the gospel we know is the essence of conversion. We can be constant and true to many worthwhile things, but ultimately we must be converted unto the Lord and the things that are spiritually and eternally essential. We should both know the gospel is true and constantly be true to the gospel.

Testimony, Conversion, and Two Parables

Two parables further emphasize the vital connection between personal testimony and ongoing conversion.

The Parable of the Ten Virgins

The oil in the familiar parable of the ten virgins has been characterized as taking the Holy Spirit for our guide (see Doctrine and Covenants 45:56–57; Neal A. Maxwell, *We Will Prove Them Herewith,* 21), making the Holy Ghost our constant companion (see Bruce R. McConkie, *The Millennial Messiah,* 343), and keeping the commandments (see *The Teachings of Harold B. Lee,* 146). Yet another way to think about this parable is to consider the lamps used by the virgins as the lamp of testimony and the oil as the oil of conversion.

"Then shall the kingdom of heaven be likened unto ten virgins, which took their lamps [of testimony], and went forth to meet the bridegroom.

"And five of them were wise, and five were foolish.

"They that were foolish took their lamps [of testimony], and took no oil [of conversion] with them."

"But the wise took oil [of conversion] in their vessels with their lamps [of testimony].

"While the bridegroom tarried, they all slumbered and slept.

"And at midnight there was a cry made, Behold, the bridegroom cometh; go ye out to meet him.

"Then all those virgins arose, and trimmed their lamps [of testimony].

"And the foolish said unto the wise, Give us of your oil [even the oil of conversion]; for our lamps [of testimony are weak and] are gone out.

"But the wise answered, saying, Not so; lest there be not enough for us and you: but go ye rather to them that sell, and buy for yourselves" (Matthew 25:1–9).

Were the five wise virgins selfish and stingy and unwilling to share? I do not believe so. Rather, they were wisely indicating that the oil of conversion cannot be borrowed from someone else. Can the spiritual strength that results from consistent and heartfelt obedience to the commandments and acting in doctrine quickly be conveyed from one person to another? Can the knowledge obtained through diligent study and pondering of the scriptures instantly be given from one who is faithful to one who is in need? Can the peace the gospel brings suddenly be transferred from a stalwart Latter-day Saint to an individual experiencing adversity or great challenge? The clear answer to each of these questions is "no."

As the wise virgins properly stated, each of us must "buy for ourselves." These inspired women were not talking about a business transaction that requires money; rather, they were describing our individual responsibility to increase the light of testimony that shines from our lamps and to obtain an ample supply of the oil of conversion unto the Lord. This precious oil is acquired one drop at a time—patiently and persistently over time. No shortcut is available; no last-minute flurry of preparation is possible. We add the oil of conversion to our lamps of testimony "line upon line, [and] precept upon precept" (2 Nephi 28:30).

"And while they went to buy, the bridegroom came; and they that were ready went in with him to the marriage: and the door was shut.

"Afterward came also the other virgins, saying, Lord, Lord, open to us.

"But he answered and said, Verily I say unto you, I know you not.

NOTES

"Watch therefore, for ye know neither the day nor the hour wherein the Son of man cometh" (Matthew 25:10–13).

As we are faithful in making, remembering, and honoring sacred covenants, then our lamps of testimony will be trimmed and burning, and we will have an ample supply of the oil of conversion.

"Wherefore, be faithful, praying always, having your lamps trimmed and burning, and oil with you, that you may be ready at the coming of the Bridegroom—

"For behold, verily, verily, I say unto you, that I come quickly. Even so. Amen" (Doctrine and Covenants 33:17–18).

See DVD Segment 7

The Parable of the Pearl and the Box

"A merchant man seeking precious jewels found at last the perfect pearl. He had the finest craftsman carve a superb jewel box and line it with blue velvet. He put his pearl of great price on display so others could share his treasure. He watched as people came to see it. Soon he turned away in sorrow. It was the box they admired, not the pearl" (Boyd K. Packer, "The Cloven Tongues of Fire," 7).

As we are learning to live the principles of the gospel of Jesus Christ, looking "beyond the mark" (Jacob 4:14) can cause us to focus incorrectly on the jewel box instead of the precious pearl of great price. For example, the Conference Center in Salt Lake City is an impressive facility, but it is a jewel box. The teachings of the living prophets and apostles, the Seventy, the Presiding Bishopric, and the general auxiliary leaders that originate from the Conference Center are the pearl of great price.

"What I the Lord have spoken, I have spoken, and I excuse not myself; and though the heavens and the earth pass away, my word shall not pass away, but shall all be fulfilled, whether by mine own voice or by the voice of my servants, it is the same" (Doctrine and Covenants 1:38).

"And whatsoever they shall speak when moved upon by the Holy Ghost shall be scripture, shall be the will of the Lord, shall be the mind of the Lord, shall be the word of the Lord, shall be the voice of the Lord, and the power of God unto salvation" (Doctrine and Covenants 68:4).

The physical structure and grounds of a temple are majestic and beautifully maintained. Indeed, the Church goes to great lengths to create a physical environment in and around a temple that appropriately invites the Spirit of the Lord. However, we should remember that the ordinances and covenants we receive in the house of the Lord are the pearl of great price. The attractive physical setting is the jewel box.

"Organize yourselves; prepare every needful thing; and establish a house, even a house of prayer, a house of fasting, a house of faith, a house of learning, a house of glory, a house of order, a house of God" (Doctrine and Covenants 88:119).

"And verily I say unto you, let this house be built unto my name, that I may reveal mine ordinances therein unto my people" (Doctrine and Covenants 124:40).

Meetings are important gatherings, but meetings in and of themselves are a jewel box. The faith, unity, worship, and edification that derive from meetings as they are directed by the Holy Ghost (see Doctrine and Covenants 46:2) are the pearl of great price.

"And their meetings were conducted by the church after the manner of the workings of the Spirit, and by the power of the Holy Ghost; for as the power of the Holy Ghost led them whether to preach, or to exhort, or to pray, or to supplicate, or to sing, even so it was done" (Moroni 6:9).

"But notwithstanding those things which are written, it always has been given to the elders of my church from the beginning, and ever shall be, to conduct all meetings as they are directed and guided by the Holy Spirit" (Doctrine and Covenants 46:2).

The programs and procedures of the Church are a jewel box; the love of God and of our fellowmen, the spiritual strength, and the individual growth realized through serving in the programs and following correct procedures are the pearl of great price.

"And the King shall answer and say unto them, Verily I say unto you, Inasmuch as ye have done it unto one of the least of these my brethren, ye have done it unto me" (Matthew 25:40).

"And behold, I tell you these things that ye may learn wisdom; that ye may learn that when ye are in the service of your fellow beings ye are only in the service of your God" (Mosiah 2:17).

Our testimonies grow and our conversion unto the Lord becomes "firm and steadfast" (Helaman 15:8) as we press forward "with an eye single to the glory of God" (Doctrine and Covenants 4:5). Indeed, the fundamental doctrines, principles, ordinances, and covenants of the restored gospel of Jesus Christ are the ultimate pearl of great price upon which we should focus.

The Importance and Power
of the Sacrament

For most of us, the turn away from self and to the Lord that constitutes "putting off the natural man" is not an immediate, smooth, continuous, and uninterrupted about-face. Rather, we are likely to start and stop, to stumble, and to both press forward and slide backward along the strait and narrow path. We may be disappointed at our apparent lack of progress or disheartened by the gap between what we know and what we actually do.

Devoted discipleship is rigorous and rewarding, exacting and edifying, and demanding and liberating. Sometimes during our mortal journey we may simply think we are incapable of making it to the final destination—that the distance we need to travel and the requirements we must fulfill are just too much. But learning and living the gospel of Jesus Christ is not hard. What truly is hard is failing to live in harmony with the truths of the restored gospel and facing the consequences of allowing the "natural man" to rule our lives. Selfishness always leads to shallow satisfaction and sorrow and renders unattainable the deepest yearnings of the soul.

As we strive to reduce the disparity between what we know and what we do, we are fortified by the knowledge that through the Atonement we can receive grace, mercy, and assurance. These blessings enable us to do good and become better than we ever could if we were relying only on our limited mortal capacity. We do not prepare for and make the trip to eternity alone.

"If ye love me, keep my commandments.

"And I will pray the Father, and he shall give you another Comforter, that he may abide with you for ever;

"Even the Spirit of truth; whom the world cannot receive,

because it seeth him not, neither knoweth him: but ye know him; for he dwelleth with you, and shall be in you.

"I will not leave you comfortless: I will come to you" (John 14:15–18).

During their ministry among the Lamanites, the sons of Mosiah encountered many challenges and much strong opposition. They too wondered if they could fulfill the weighty responsibilities associated with their callings.

"Now do ye remember, my brethren, that we said unto our brethren in the land of Zarahemla, we go up to the land of Nephi, to preach unto our brethren, the Lamanites, and they laughed us to scorn?

"For they said unto us: Do ye suppose that ye can bring the Lamanites to the knowledge of the truth? Do ye suppose that ye can convince the Lamanites of the incorrectness of the traditions of their fathers, as stiffnecked a people as they are; whose hearts delight in the shedding of blood; whose days have been spent in the grossest iniquity; whose ways have been the ways of a transgressor from the beginning? Now my brethren, ye remember that this was their language.

"And moreover they did say: Let us take up arms against them, that we destroy them and their iniquity out of the land, lest they overrun us and destroy us.

"But behold, my beloved brethren, we came into the wilderness not with the intent to destroy our brethren, but with the intent that perhaps we might save some few of their souls.

"Now *when our hearts were depressed, and we were about to turn back, behold, the Lord comforted us,* and said: Go amongst thy brethren, the Lamanites, and bear with patience thine afflictions, and I will give unto you success" (Alma 26:23–27; emphasis added).

These faithful missionaries were blessed with comfort, with increased spiritual capacity and stamina, and with success. And the same promises are true for you and me today and are available to us through the sacred ordinance of the sacrament.

We participate in the ordinance of the sacrament in remembrance of the Atonement of Jesus Christ. The broken bread represents His broken flesh; the water represents the blood that He shed to atone for our sins (see 1 Corinthians 11:23–25; Doctrine and Covenants 27:2). Through this ordinance, Church members renew their baptismal covenants and can be blessed with the spiritual assurance, correction, and direction needed to continue steadfastly turning away from self and to the Lord.

The Lord initiated the sacrament anciently as He participated in the Passover meal with His Apostles (see Matthew 26:17–28).

"And as they were eating, Jesus took bread, and blessed it, and brake it, and gave it to the disciples, and said, Take, eat; this is my body.

"And he took the cup, and gave thanks, and gave it to them, saying, Drink ye all of it;

"For this is my blood of the new testament, which is shed for many for the remission of sins" (Matthew 26:26–28).

The resurrected Savior again emphasized the importance of the sacrament when He visited the American continent and instituted this ordinance among the faithful Nephites. He blessed the emblems of the sacrament and gave them to His disciples and the multitude (see 3 Nephi 18:1–10).

"And this shall ye always do to those who repent and are baptized in my name; and ye shall do it in remembrance of my blood, which I have shed for you, that ye may witness unto the Father that ye do always remember me. And if ye do always remember me ye shall have my Spirit to be with you.

" . . . And if ye shall always do these things blessed are ye, for ye are built upon my rock.

"But whoso among you shall do more or less than these are not built upon my rock, but are built upon a sandy foundation; and when the rain descends, and the floods come, and the winds blow, and beat upon them, they shall fall" (3 Nephi 18:11–13).

The sacrament is the ordinance that replaced the blood sacrifices and burnt offerings of the Mosaic law. The Savior promised: "And whoso cometh unto me with a broken heart and a contrite spirit, him will I baptize with fire and with the Holy Ghost" (3 Nephi 9:20).

Conscientiously preparing for and worthily partaking of the sacramental emblems help us to (1) review regularly where we are in turning away from self and toward the Savior, (2) reorient ourselves to the "weightier matters of the law" (Matthew 23:23)—the pearl of great price instead of the jewel box, (3) make necessary course corrections along the strait and narrow path (see 2 Nephi 31:18), and (4) seek appropriately for the blessings and spiritual gifts we need in our lives to continue as we commenced.

"Examine yourselves, whether ye be in the faith; prove your own selves" (2 Corinthians 13:5).

Consider the primary purposes of the Lord's Supper as described in the early days of the latter-day dispensation in which we live.

"And *that thou mayest more fully keep thyself unspotted from the world,* thou shalt go to the house of prayer and offer up thy sacraments upon my holy day;

"For verily this is a day appointed unto you to rest from your labors, and to pay thy devotions unto the Most High;

"Nevertheless thy vows shall be offered up in righteousness on all days and at all times;

"But remember that on this, the Lord's day, thou shalt offer thine oblations and thy sacraments unto the Most High, confessing thy sins unto thy brethren, and before the Lord" (Doctrine and Covenants 59:9–12; emphasis added).

As members of the Savior's restored Church, we take part in the ordinance of the sacrament more frequently than any other ordinance—and we can receive recurring assistance to more fully keep ourselves unspotted from the world. Given the increasing wickedness and darkness in the world in which we live, we truly are blessed to participate in this ordinance in our regular Sabbath meetings.

Elder Melvin J. Ballard testified of the healing and comforting power of the sacrament: "I am a witness that there is a spirit attending the administration of the sacrament that warms the soul from head to foot; you feel the wounds of the spirit being healed, and the load is lifted. Comfort and happiness come to the soul that is worthy and truly desirous of partaking of this spiritual food" ("The Sacramental Covenant," 1027).

The ordinance of the sacrament is one of the greatest influences in our lives to reduce the disparity between what we know and what we do. We are reminded of and renew again each week the pledge of our willingness to take upon ourselves the name of Jesus Christ, to follow Him, to remember Him, to keep His commandments, and to emulate His character. We recommit every time we partake of the bread and the water that we are willing to keep working, striving, repenting, and improving. And when we rely upon His merits, mercy, and grace (see 2 Nephi 2:8), our confidence increases that "in the strength of the Lord [we can] do all things" (Alma 20:4).

Receiving and retaining a remission of our sins are essential if we are to have an eye single to the glory of God and the constant companionship of the Holy Ghost. King Benjamin powerfully taught his people about the need for heartfelt repentance—of returning to and depending upon the Lord.

"And again, believe that ye must repent of your sins and forsake them, and humble yourselves before God; and ask in sincerity of heart that he would forgive you; and now, *if you believe all these things see that ye do them.*

"And again I say unto you as I have said before, that as ye have come to the knowledge of the glory of God, or if ye have known of his goodness and have tasted of his love, and have received a remission of your sins, which causeth such exceedingly great joy in your souls, even so I would that ye should remember, and always retain in remembrance, the greatness of God, and your own nothingness, and his goodness and long-suffering towards you, unworthy creatures, and humble yourselves even in the depths of humility, calling on the name of the Lord daily, and standing steadfastly in the faith of that which is to come, which was spoken by the mouth of the angel.

"And behold, I say unto you that *if ye do this ye shall always rejoice,* and be filled with the love of God, and always retain a remission of your sins; and ye shall grow in the knowledge of the glory of him that created you, or in the knowledge of that which is just and true" (Mosiah 4:10–12; emphasis added).

The sacrament is a frequent and consistent focal point for our repentance, our spiritual renewal and development, and our continued turning to the Savior. Note that as Jesus instituted the sacrament among the Nephites, He sent the disciples to bring the emblems for this sacred ordinance.

"*And while they were gone for bread and wine,* he commanded the multitude that they should sit themselves down upon the earth" (3 Nephi 18:2; emphasis added).

Interestingly, the Savior had on other occasions provided at His word fishes and loaves for the multitude (see Matthew 14:15–21; Matthew 15:32–38; Luke 9:10–17). And He certainly could have supplied instantly the needed bread and wine. But instead He invited the multitude to sit upon the ground—perhaps so they would have time to contemplate what they have been taught and to prepare for the sacrament. This emphasis upon appropriate introspection and pondering before and during this ordinance are particularly important for us today as we strive to reduce the disparity between what we know and what we do.

Recognizing that we are not now perfect and that the perfection we are commanded to achieve (see Matthew 5:48; 3 Nephi 12:48) will not be realized in mortality, the sacrament is an essential element in the "line upon line, precept upon precept, here a little and there a little " (2 Nephi 28:30) progress we can be blessed to accomplish.

"Nevertheless they did fast and pray oft, and did wax stronger and stronger in their humility, and firmer and firmer in the faith of Christ, unto the filling their souls with joy and consolation, yea, even to the purifying and the sanctification of their hearts, which sanctification cometh because of their yielding their hearts unto God" (Helaman 3:35).

THE POWER OF TEMPLE COVENANTS

An additional source of strength as we steadfastly turn to the Savior is found in the making and keeping of temple covenants. Here again, the level of our commitment and understanding will significantly affect the blessings we are privileged to receive.

For many years Sister Bednar and I hosted faithful men and women as devotional speakers at Brigham Young University–Idaho.

Many of these speakers were emeritus or released members of the Seventy who had served as temple presidents following their service as General Authorities. As we talked with these stalwart leaders, I always asked this question: "What have you learned as a temple president that you wish you had better understood when you were a General Authority?"

As I listened to their answers, I discovered a consistent theme that I would summarize as follows: "I have come to understand better the protection available through our temple covenants and what it means to make an acceptable offering of temple worship. There is a difference between church-attending, tithe-paying members who occasionally rush into the temple to go through a session and those members who faithfully and consistently worship in the temple."

To me this episode highlights the difference between testimony (knowing that we ought to go to the temple) and conversion (worshiping with devotion in a meaningful way in the temple).

The adversary will do everything he can to discourage a deeper level of conversion to our temple covenants. We should not be surprised by his efforts to thwart or discredit temple worship and work. The devil despises the purity in and the power of the Lord's house. And the protection available to each of us in and through temple ordinances and covenants stands as a great obstacle to the evil designs of Lucifer.

The power of temple covenants has been evident throughout the history of the restored Church. For example, the exodus from Nauvoo in September of 1846 caused unimaginable hardship for the faithful Latter-day Saints. Many sought shelter in camps along the Mississippi River. When word reached Brigham Young at Winter Quarters about the condition of these refugees, he immediately sent a letter across the river to Council Point encouraging the brethren to help—reminding them of the covenant made in the Nauvoo Temple. He counseled: "Now is the time for labor. Let the fire of the covenant which you made in the House of the Lord, burn in your hearts, like flame unquenchable" (in *Journal History of The Church of Jesus Christ of Latter-day Saints,* September 28, 1846, 5). Within days, wagons were rolling eastward to rescue the struggling Saints.

What was it that gave those early Saints such strength? It was the fire of the temple covenant that burned in their hearts.

We do now and will yet face great challenges to the work of the Lord. But like the pioneers who found the place which God for them prepared, so we will fresh courage take, knowing our God will never us forsake (see "Come, Come, Ye Saints," *Hymns,* no. 30). Today temples dot the earth as sacred places of ordinances and covenants, of edification, and of refuge from the storm.

SUMMARY

Obtaining a testimony, becoming converted, and participating worthily in the ordinances of the sacrament and the temple are key components in turning away from self and to the Lord. As we come to a knowledge of the truth, are converted unto the Lord, and honor and remember sacred covenants, then the promised blessing is that we never will fall away. We eagerly will set aside the weapons of rebellion in our lives. Our turn to the Lord and away from self will be "steadfast and immovable" (Mosiah 5:15). And our capacity to live more in alignment with what we know will be enlarged.

By divine design, discipleship is demanding. We are admonished to serve the Lord with all of our heart, might, mind, and strength (see Doctrine and Covenants 4:2). We are required to

NOTES

See DVD Segment 17

"offer [our] whole [soul] as an offering unto him, and continue in fasting and praying, and endure to the end" (Omni 1:26). But only as we expend our moral agency to conform our lives to His will and timing—as we lose our life for His sake—can we ultimately find it (see Matthew 10:37–39).

"And moreover, I would desire that ye should consider on the blessed and happy state of those that keep the commandments of God. For behold, they are blessed in all things, both temporal and spiritual; and if they hold out faithful to the end they are received into heaven, that thereby they may dwell with God in a state of never-ending happiness. O remember, remember that these things are true; for the Lord God hath spoken it" (Mosiah 2:41).

RELATED READINGS FOR CHAPTER THREE

The two related readings for Chapter Three focus upon the Lord's principal pattern for spiritual development.

"For behold, thus saith the Lord God: I will give unto the children of men line upon line, precept upon precept, here a little and there a little; and blessed are those who hearken unto my precepts, and lend an ear unto my counsel, for they shall learn wisdom; for unto him that receiveth I will give more; and from them that shall say, We have enough, from them shall be taken away even that which they have" (2 Nephi 28:30).

"By Small and Simple Things Are Great Things Brought to Pass"
BYU Women's Conference, April 2011;
available online at http://ce.byu.edu/cw/womensconference
/archive/2011/pdf/Elder_David_A._Bednar.pdf

Steady, sustained, and incremental spiritual progress produces the fruit of steadfastness—and helps us to reduce the disparity between what we know and what we do. Testimony is strengthened and conversion unto the Lord is deepened through small and simple things done well over time.

"Who's on the Lord's Side? Now Is the Time to Show"
BYU–Idaho Education Week, July 2010;
available online at http://www2.byui.edu/Presentations
/Transcripts/EducationWeek/2010_07_30_Bednar.htm

The grand combination of many seemingly small choices and actions provides the conclusive answer to the question of "Who's on the Lord's side?"

CONSIDER

What can and should I do to strengthen my testimony of God the Eternal Father and of His Son Jesus Christ?

CONSIDER

What am I learning about the relationship between testimony and conversion that can help me reduce the disparity between what I know and what I do?

Consider

What can and should I do in my life to lay down my weapons of rebellion?

CONSIDER

What can and should I do to more fully understand and appreciate the power of ordinances and covenants in my life?

CONSIDER

What can and should I do in my life to make the ordinance of the sacrament an ongoing part of turning to the Lord—of putting off the natural man and becoming a saint through the Atonement of Jesus Christ?

MY OWN QUESTIONS TO CONSIDER

Scriptures Related to What I Am Learning

Scriptures Related to What I Am Learning

AN INVITATION TO LEARN AND ACT		
What additional doctrines and principles, if understood, would help me strengthen my testimony and become more fully converted?	What can and should I do to "act in" those doctrines and principles?	How will I know if I am making progress in becoming a converted disciple of the Savior?

AN INVITATION TO LEARN AND ACT		
What additional doctrines and principles, if understood, would help me strengthen my testimony and become more fully converted?	What can and should I do to "act in" those doctrines and principles?	How will I know if I am making progress in becoming a converted disciple of the Savior?

AN INVITATION TO LEARN AND ACT		
What additional doctrines and principles, if understood, would help me strengthen my testimony and become more fully converted?	What can and should I do to "act in" those doctrines and principles?	How will I know if I am making progress in becoming a converted disciple of the Savior?

_____

_____

_____

_____

_____

_____

_____

_____

_____

_____

_____

_____

CHAPTER FOUR

Acting in Doctrine and the Role of a Teacher

As we turn resolutely to the Savior, we are blessed with "a love of God and *of all men*" (2 Nephi 31:20; emphasis added) and are drawn to serve our brothers and sisters. The natural consequence of coming unto Christ with real intent and striving to be perfected in Him (see Moroni 10:32) is turning outward in service and compassion.

Turning and Serving

Lehi's vision provides an excellent example of how service flows from devoted discipleship. The central feature in Lehi's dream is the tree of life—which is a representation of "the love of God" (1 Nephi 11:21–22).

"For God so loved the world, that he gave his only begotten Son, that whosoever believeth in him should not perish, but have everlasting life" (John 3:16).

The birth, life, and atoning sacrifice of the Lord Jesus Christ are the greatest manifestations of God's love for His children. As

111

Nephi testifies, this love is "most desirable above all things" and "most joyous to the soul" (1 Nephi 11:22–23; see also 1 Nephi 8:12, 15). Chapter eleven of First Nephi presents a detailed description of the tree of life as a symbol for the life, ministry, and sacrifice of the Savior—the "condescension of God" (1 Nephi 11:16). The tree can be considered a representation of Christ.

One way of thinking about the fruit on the tree is as a symbol for the blessings of the Atonement. Partaking of the fruit of the tree may represent the receiving of ordinances and covenants whereby the Atonement can become fully efficacious in our lives. The fruit is described as "desirable to make one happy" (1 Nephi 8:10) and produces great joy and the desire to share that joy with others.

"And it came to pass that I beheld a tree, whose fruit was desirable to make one happy.

"And it came to pass that I did go forth and partake of the fruit thereof; and I beheld that it was most sweet, above all that I ever before tasted. Yea, and I beheld that the fruit thereof was white, to exceed all the whiteness that I had ever seen.

"And as I partook of the fruit thereof it filled my soul with exceedingly great joy; wherefore, *I began to be desirous that my family should partake of it also;* for I knew that it was desirable above all other fruit" (1 Nephi 8:10–12; emphasis added).

Lehi's instinctive and immediate response to partaking of the fruit of the tree and experiencing great joy was an increased desire to serve his family. Thus, as he turned to Christ he also turned outward in service.

Enos was blessed in a similar way as his pleading petition to God was heard and answered.

"And I will tell you of the wrestle which I had before God, before I received a remission of my sins.

"Behold, I went to hunt beasts in the forests; and the words which I had often heard my father speak concerning eternal life, and the joy of the saints, sunk deep into my heart.

"And my soul hungered; and I kneeled down before my Maker, and I cried unto him in mighty prayer and supplication for mine own soul; and all the day long did I cry unto him; yea, and when the night came I did still raise my voice high that it reached the heavens.

"And there came a voice unto me, saying: Enos, thy sins are forgiven thee, and thou shalt be blessed.

"And I, Enos, knew that God could not lie; wherefore, my guilt was swept away.

"And I said: Lord, how is it done?

"And he said unto me: Because of thy faith in Christ, whom thou hast never before heard nor seen. And many years pass away before he shall manifest himself in the flesh; wherefore, go to, thy faith hath made thee whole.

"Now, it came to pass that *when I had heard these words I began to feel a desire for the welfare of my brethren, the Nephites; wherefore, I did pour out my whole soul unto God for them*" (Enos 1:2–9; emphasis added).

As Enos turned to the Lord "with full purpose of heart" (2 Nephi 31:13), his concern for the welfare of his family, friends, and associates increased almost simultaneously.

One of the enduring lessons we should learn from these two poignant episodes is the importance of experiencing in our own lives the blessings of the Atonement as a prerequisite to the kind of service that stretches far beyond merely "going through the motions." Acting in doctrine precedes serving "with all [of our] heart, might, mind and strength" (Doctrine and Covenants 4:2).

Testimony and conversion are the basis for authentic Christian service in our homes, in the Church, and in our communities.

Alma's personal experience with the mighty change of heart is reflected in his powerful preaching and the questions he posed to the people in the Church in the city of Zarahemla.

"And now behold, I ask of you, my brethren of the church, have ye spiritually been born of God? Have ye received his image in your countenances? Have ye experienced this mighty change in your hearts? . . .

"And now behold, I say unto you, my brethren, if ye have experienced a change of heart, and if ye have felt to sing the song of redeeming love, I would ask, can ye feel so now?" (Alma 5:14, 26).

Alma obviously had learned the lyrics to the song of redeeming love long before he preached this sermon. He was not simply presenting a message or "giving a talk" to the members of the Church; he was communicating truth from the depths of his heart and by the power of the Spirit.

The examples of Lehi, Enos, and Alma affirm the truth that as we turn to the Savior, we also become anxiously engaged in serving, supporting, and sustaining Heavenly Father's sons and daughters. As we "come to the knowledge of the glory of God, [know] of his goodness and [taste] of his love, [and receive] a remission of [our] sins," then we will "always rejoice," "be filled with the love of God," "retain a remission of [our] sins," "grow in the knowledge" of God and "of that which is just and true," "render to every man according to that which is his due," teach our children "to walk in the ways of truth and soberness" and "to love . . . and to serve one another," and "succor those that stand in need of [our] succor" and "administer of [our]substance unto him that standeth in need" (Mosiah 4:11–16).

Thus, the selfishness of the natural man is replaced by the

selflessness of a saint as we turn to the Lord and invite into our lives the rich blessings of His infinite and eternal Atonement.

TEACHING IS SERVING

Every person who enters into sacred covenants and becomes a member of The Church of Jesus Christ of Latter-day Saints is a teacher—at all times and in all places. Teaching is one of the most important types of service we can render in our homes and in the Church because helping others to learn and live gospel truths is eternally important and personally edifying.

"And I give unto you a commandment that you shall *teach one another* the doctrine of the kingdom.

"*Teach ye diligently* and my grace shall attend you, that you may be instructed more perfectly in theory, in principle, in doctrine, in the law of the gospel, in all things that pertain unto the kingdom of God, that are expedient for you to understand" (Doctrine and Covenants 88:77–78; emphasis added).

"And as all have not faith, seek ye diligently and *teach one another* words of wisdom; yea, seek ye out of the best books words of wisdom; seek learning, even by study and also by faith" (Doctrine and Covenants 88:118; emphasis added).

"And again, inasmuch as parents have children in Zion, or in any of her stakes which are organized, that *teach them not to understand* the doctrine of repentance, faith in Christ the Son of the living God, and of baptism and the gift of the Holy Ghost by the laying on of the hands, when eight years old, the sin be upon the heads of the parents. . . .

"And they shall also *teach their children* to pray, and to walk uprightly before the Lord" (Doctrine and Covenants 68:25, 28; emphasis added).

Many people typically associate teaching with talking, telling, lecturing, and explaining in a formal setting like a classroom. And certainly these important functions are involved in teaching. But we should always remember that the Holy Ghost is the ultimate and true teacher—not us. The Spirit of the Lord can enter into a learner's heart, when invited through sincere desire and faithful acting in doctrine, and will confirm the truthfulness of the gospel principles that person is endeavoring to understand and live. Indeed, you and I as teachers have the responsibility to preach the gospel by the Spirit, even the Comforter, as a prerequisite for the learning by faith that is obtained only by and through the Holy Ghost (see Doctrine and Covenants 50:14). But the lessons we teach and the testimonies we bear are preparatory to a learner's acting and learning for himself or herself.

Parents as Teachers

As with most principles of the gospel, effective teaching begins in the home. Parents need to recognize their crucial role in helping their children learn by the power of the Holy Ghost and turn from self to the Savior.

The importance and lasting influence of parents as teachers is dramatically evidenced in a story Elder L. Tom Perry has told about an ancestor of his, Gustavus Adolphus Perry, the first member of the Perry family to join The Church of Jesus Christ of Latter-day Saints (see "The Value of a Good Name," 179–85). Gustavus, his wife, Eunice, and their seven children lived on a beautiful farm in upstate New York. The Perry family first heard the message of the restored gospel in 1830 and was baptized in 1832. After joining the Church, the family moved from New York to Ohio, from Ohio to Missouri, from Missouri to Illinois, and from Illinois across the plains to the Great Salt Lake Valley. The town of Perry, Utah, is named after the oldest son of Gustavus and Eunice, the first bishop to serve in that community.

In 1997, the Perry family celebrated the two-hundredth birthday of Gustavus Perry. In preparation for that celebration, Elder L. Tom Perry's brother conducted extensive research and identified as many of the descendants of Gustavus and Eunice as he could. Can you guess the number of descendants Elder Perry's brother found?

The answer—more than ten thousand family members had come from this faithful man and woman.

Elder Perry stated in his devotional message: "The number overwhelmed me. I could not believe that there could be more than 10,000 descendants of Gustavus Adolphus Perry. . . . In seven to eight generations, his family had sufficient numbers to organize three stakes of [the Church]" ("The Value of a Good Name," 180).

In this illustration we witness the power of a faithful husband and wife who did their best to rear children in righteousness: testimony of and conversion to Christ endured across the generations to grandchildren, great-grandchildren, and thousands more. Many seemingly ordinary family prayers, common experiences working together, gospel conversations, tragedies and triumphs, and meaningful Sabbath days in scores of families across the generations produced a legacy of faithfulness.

We can begin preparing the hearts of our family members to be taught by telling the people we love that we love them. Such expressions do not need to be flowery or lengthy. We simply should sincerely and frequently express love. Love is a gift of the Spirit and also a fruit thereof, and as such it is an important component in gospel teaching.

When was the last time you took your eternal companion in your arms and said, "I love you"? When was the last time you sincerely expressed love to your children or to your parents?

Each of us already knows we should tell the people we love that we love them. But what we know is not always reflected in what we do. We may feel unsure, awkward, or even perhaps a bit embarrassed. As disciples of the Savior, we are not merely striving to know more; rather, we need to consistently do more of what we know is right and become better.

We should remember that saying "I love you" is only a beginning. We need to say it, we need to mean it, and, most important, we need consistently to show it. We need to both express and demonstrate love.

President Thomas S. Monson has counseled: "Often we assume that [the people around us] *must* know how much we love them. But we should never assume; we should let them know. . . . We will never regret the kind words spoken or the affection shown. Rather, our regrets will come if such things are omitted from our relationships with those who mean the most to us" ("Finding Joy in the Journey," 86).

We also can become more effective teachers at home by bearing testimony to those whom we love about the things we know to be true by the witness of the Holy Ghost. The bearing of testimony need not be lengthy or eloquent. And we do not need to wait until the first Sunday of the month to declare our witness of things that are true. Within the walls of our own homes, we can and should bear pure testimony of the divinity and reality of the Father and the Son, of the great plan of happiness, and of the Restoration.

The relationship between testimony and appropriate action

that teaches is emphasized in the Savior's instruction to the Saints in Kirtland: "That which the Spirit testifies unto you even so I would that ye should do" (Doctrine and Covenants 46:7). Our testimony of gospel truth should be reflected both in our words and in our deeds. And our testimonies are proclaimed and lived most powerfully in our own homes. Spouses, parents, and children should strive to overcome any hesitancy, reluctance, or embarrassment about bearing testimony. We should both create and look for opportunities to bear testimony of gospel truths—and live them.

As our sons were growing up, our family did what you have done and what you now do. We had regular family prayer, scripture study, and family home evening. Sometimes Sister Bednar and I wondered if our efforts to do these spiritually essential things were worthwhile. Now and then verses of scripture were read amid outbursts such as "He's touching me!" "Make him stop looking at me!" "Mom, he's breathing my air!" Sincere prayers occasionally were interrupted with giggling and poking. And with active, rambunctious boys, family home evening lessons did not always produce high levels of edification. At times Sister Bednar and I were exasperated because the righteous habits we worked so hard to foster did not seem to yield immediately the spiritual results we wanted and expected.

Today if you could ask our adult sons what they remember about family prayer, scripture study, and family home evening, I believe I know how they would answer. They likely would not identify a particular prayer or a specific instance of scripture study or an especially meaningful family home evening lesson as the defining moment in their spiritual development. What they would say they remember is that as a family we were consistent.

Sister Bednar and I thought helping our sons understand the content of a particular lesson or a specific scripture was the

See DVD Segment 6

ultimate outcome. But such a result does not occur each time we study or pray or learn together. The consistency of our intent and work was perhaps the greatest lesson—a lesson we did not fully appreciate at the time.

In my office is a beautiful painting of a wheat field. The painting is a vast collection of individual brushstrokes—none of which in isolation is very interesting or impressive. In fact, if you stand close to the canvas, all you can see is a mass of seemingly unrelated and unattractive streaks of yellow and gold and brown paint. However, as you gradually move away from the canvas, all of the individual brushstrokes combine together and produce a magnificent landscape of a wheat field. Many ordinary, individual brushstrokes work together to create a captivating and beautiful painting.

Each family prayer, each episode of family scripture study, and each family home evening is a brushstroke on the canvas of our souls. No one event may appear to be very impressive or memorable. But just as the yellow and gold and brown strokes of paint complement each other and produce an impressive masterpiece, so our consistency in doing seemingly small things can lead to significant spiritual results. "Wherefore, be not weary in well-doing, for ye are laying the foundation of a great work. And out of small things proceedeth that which is great" (Doctrine and Covenants 64:33). Consistency is a key principle as we lay the foundation of a great work in our individual lives and as we accept our responsibility to become teachers in our own homes.

ACTING IN DOCTRINE AND TEACHING

Two rather simple but profound experiences have influenced greatly my understanding about the relationship between acting in doctrine and the role of a teacher. Interestingly, both experiences involved President Boyd K. Packer and Elder Neal A. Maxwell.

Experience #1—Please Teach Us about the Atonement

In 1995 I was called to serve as an Area Authority in the North America Southwest area of The Church of Jesus Christ of Latter-day Saints. Because we were entering a new era of Church leadership and administration through the elimination of the office of Regional Representative, all of the new Area Authorities in North America were requested to come to Church headquarters in Salt Lake City for training. We gathered together to receive instruction from President Boyd K. Packer and Elder Neal A. Maxwell.

As is often the case in such meetings, President Packer invited us to ask questions. I have never forgotten one question that was directed specifically to President Packer and the answer he gave.

"President Packer, would you please teach us about the Atonement of Jesus Christ?"

I was edified by the spiritual significance of the question and eager to hear the answer. President Packer then gave the following response:

"Thank you for your excellent question. Read the Book of Mormon as many times as you reasonably can in the next several months. When you are finished reading, write a one-page summary of what you learned about the Atonement. Next question."

The brevity of his answer to such an important question initially startled me. I admit to being a bit disappointed that we did not receive a detailed doctrinal response. But his answer certainly caused me to think, to ponder, to pray, and, most important, to act.

As I read the Book of Mormon repeatedly in the weeks and

months that followed that memorable meeting and wrote my one-page summary of the doctrine of the Atonement, and as I repeated that process many times in the ensuing years, I reflected often on President Packer's invitation. I have come to understand that he gave us much more than an answer to a single question. In that training session he did not tell us what he knew; rather, he taught us how he had come to know. If any of us truly desired to know what he knew, we absolutely could—if we were willing to pay the price and obtain the knowledge for ourselves. President Packer's answer emphasized the importance of procuring for ourselves the oil of conversion; it cannot be borrowed or conveyed from one person to another.

We in that first group of Area Authorities perhaps mistakenly had hoped that President Packer would transfer to us all he had learned through a lifetime of study about the Savior's Atonement. But he had helped us learn that knowledge cannot be given or borrowed; it must be obtained. He had, as a teacher, invited us to be agents who act and not objects that are acted upon. And he directed us to the pathway we needed to pursue if we were to obtain "great treasures of knowledge, even hidden treasures" (Doctrine and Covenants 89:19).

The importance of this lesson was reaffirmed in a powerful way in my own family. One of our sons was serving as a full-time missionary at the time that first training meeting for Area Authorities took place. In a letter to our son, I described what I had observed and learned and suggested that he should consider responding to President Packer's instruction.

Many months later Susan and I received a letter from our missionary son. Inside the envelope we found an additional treasure—a one-page, typed summary of the doctrine of the Atonement. Our hearts were filled with gratitude as we realized what our son was learning during his personal study time as a missionary—without a lesson manual, without a classroom teacher to support and direct him, without an outline of learning objectives, and without visual aids or video segments. He had the Book of Mormon, the Holy Ghost, a piece of paper, and a keyboard.

After reading our son's summary, I simply said to Susan, "I wish I had understood the Atonement as well when I was a missionary." And together we gained an even greater appreciation for the power of the Lord's pattern of learning.

Experience #2—Inspired Teaching about Teaching

The first chapter of this book focuses upon the character of Christ and how His attributes and perfections should form the foundation of our faith in Him. The teachings of Elder Neal A. Maxwell sparked my initial interest in this spiritually significant and eternally important topic. How grateful I am for Elder Maxwell's prophetic insights and personal encouragement.

The final chapter of this book focuses upon acting in doctrine and the role of a teacher. The teachings of Elder Neal A. Maxwell were instrumental in helping me to think, ponder, pray, and learn in new ways about this subject as well. I pay tribute to this valiant Apostle for his extraordinary ability to present enough but not too much instruction as a teacher so as to inspire learners to become anxiously engaged in seeking for additional knowledge, understanding, and intelligence.

After my call to serve as an Area Seventy in The Church of Jesus Christ of Latter-day Saints, I was privileged to attend and participate in many training meetings. The annual gathering in Salt Lake City of all General Authorities and Area Seventies to receive counsel from the members of the First Presidency, the Quorum of the Twelve, the seven presidents of the Seventy, and the Presiding Bishopric always was my favorite. I looked forward each year with great anticipation to this remarkable opportunity to learn.

I remember vividly during one of the training sessions an invitation from President Boyd K. Packer to ask questions. I was able to ask the following question.

"President Packer, what would you teach us about teaching?"

President Packer immediately turned to Elder Maxwell and invited him to respond to my question. He came to the podium and gave this simple, succinct answer:

"Do not be afraid of repetitious teaching.

"Ask inspired questions.

"Typically, but not always, two-way dialogue is better than one-way monologue."

The three elements of Elder Maxwell's answer took no more than twenty to thirty seconds to articulate. He did not elaborate on any of the specific points of his answer. He quietly returned to his seat, and the next question was asked.

As I have reflected upon, studied about, and pondered this brief statement over the course of many years, I have concluded that it is one of the greatest discourses ever uttered about learning and teaching. Note that two of the three components identified in the answer focus upon the importance of a learner acting (responding to inspired questions; engaging in a two-way dialogue). It is in essence a summary of the Lord's pattern.

See DVD Segment 14

"Appoint among yourselves a teacher, and let not all be spokesmen at once; but let one speak at a time and let all listen unto his sayings, that when all have spoken that all may be edified of all, and that every man may have an equal privilege" (Doctrine and Covenants 88:122).

INVITING LEARNERS TO ACT

As teachers, one of our most important responsibilities is to invite learners to act—to exercise their moral agency in accordance with the teachings of the Savior.

Regardless of how worthy we are and how effectively we teach, you and I simply cannot push or force truth into the hearts of learners. Teaching, exhorting, explaining, and testifying, as important as they are, can never convey or transfer to a learner a witness of the truthfulness of the restored gospel. Our best efforts can only bring the message of truth *unto* the heart (see 2 Nephi 33:1). Ultimately, a learner needs to act in righteousness and thereby invite the truth *into* his or her own heart. Only in this way can honest seekers of truth develop the spiritual capacity to find answers for themselves—and "to stand as witnesses of God at all times and in all things, and in all places" (Mosiah 18:9).

An experience I had while participating in a priesthood leadership meeting illustrates the importance of inviting a learner to act—thereby enabling truth to penetrate into the heart. Several other General Authorities and I were assigned to teach a large group of brethren about the doctrine of the priesthood and correct principles related to their callings and duties. A portion of the meeting was used to invite and respond to questions from the participants about the topics that had been addressed. I was assigned to conduct the question-and-answer portion of the meeting.

One brother stood and asked this simple and straightforward question, "Elder Bednar, is it permissible to eat pork?" I responded by asking several questions that helped me to learn about his recent baptism and his experience as the full-time missionaries had taught him. I also asked him if he was familiar with the Doctrine and Covenants. The man indicated that he knew the Doctrine and

Covenants was a book of scripture but he had not yet read it. I suggested he would find the answer to his question in section eighty-nine of the Doctrine and Covenants and invited him to read that revelation at a later time.

Before I could solicit another question, this good brother again asked, "Elder Bednar, is it permissible to eat pork?" I promised the man that he would find his answer in section eighty-nine and started to call on another brother to ask a question. In a loud voice, the man exclaimed, "Elder Bednar, your answer is unacceptable. I simply want you to tell me if it is permissible to eat pork!" The tone of his voice and the tension in the room suggested that this particular episode might not have a happy conclusion.

I once again invited the brother to act and find his answer by reading and studying section eighty-nine. He once again requested that I answer his question. I finally said, "Dear brother, you have asked the same question several times, and I have given the same answer several times. Let's call it a draw. I do not think your question will change, and I am quite sure my answer will not change. Please read section eighty-nine of the Doctrine and Covenants so you can find for yourself the answer you need." Our exchange ended with the man having a disgusted and most unpleasant look on his face. And I wondered if I had mishandled the answering of his question and caused him unnecessary exasperation.

The next morning as I walked into the Church building where a large, multistake conference was to be held and from which the proceedings would be broadcast to many other congregations, I was approached by a Church media services employee. He excitedly indicated that he had a message for me from the man who had asked the question about eating pork in the priesthood leadership meeting. I must confess that I initially thought, *Oh no, the man wants me to know that I offended him and he is not coming back to church ever again.* Instead, I was given the following report:

"Tell Elder Bednar I got my answer. Please tell Elder Bednar that I got my answer. I read section eighty-nine—and I got my answer!"

Please notice that the man did not say, "I got an answer," or "I got the answer." Rather, he exclaimed, "I got *my* answer." His statement revealed an element of discovery and a personal ownership that truly are significant.

I have observed a common characteristic among the teachers who have had the greatest influence in my life. They have required and helped me to seek learning by faith. They refused to give me easy answers to questions. In fact, they usually did not give me any answers at all. Rather, they pointed the way and helped me take the steps to find my own answers. I certainly did not always appreciate this approach, but experience has enabled me to understand that an answer given by another person usually is not remembered for very long, if at all. But an answer we discover or obtain through the exercise of faith is typically retained for a lifetime. The most important learnings of life are caught—not taught.

The spiritual understanding you and I have been blessed to receive, and which has been confirmed as true in our hearts, simply cannot be given to another person. The tuition of diligence and learning by faith must be paid to obtain and personally "own" such knowledge. Only in this way can what is known in the mind be transformed into what is felt in the heart. Only in this way can a person move beyond relying upon the spiritual knowledge and experience of others and claim those blessings for himself or herself. Only in this way can we be spiritually prepared for what is coming.

One more example of inviting learners to act for themselves concerns an invitation I extended to the youth of the Church to assist in family history work. Many young people assume that family history work is to be performed primarily by older generations. But I know of no age limit described in the scriptures or guidelines announced by Church leaders restricting this important service to mature adults. Youth are sons and daughters of God, children of the covenant, and builders of the kingdom.

The Lord has made available in our day remarkable resources that enable anyone to learn about and love this work that is sparked by the Spirit of Elijah. For example, FamilySearch is a collection of records, resources, and services easily accessible with personal computers and a variety of handheld devices, designed to help people discover and document their family history. These resources also are available in the family history centers located in many of our Church buildings throughout the world.

It is no coincidence that FamilySearch and other tools have come forth at a time when young people are so familiar with a wide range of information and communication technologies. The skills and aptitude evident among many young people today are a preparation to contribute to the work of salvation.

Parents and leaders can help children and youth to learn about and experience the Spirit of Elijah. But do not overly program this endeavor or provide too much detailed information or training. Invite young people to explore, to experiment, and to learn for themselves (see Joseph Smith–History 1:20). Any young person can do what I am suggesting, using the modules available at lds.org/familyhistoryyouth. Aaronic Priesthood quorum and Young Women class presidencies can play an important role in helping all youth become acquainted with these basic resources. Young people increasingly need to be learners who act and thereby receive additional light and knowledge by the power of the Holy

Ghost—and not merely passive students who primarily are acted upon (see 2 Nephi 2:26).

Troy Jackson, Jaren Hope, and Andrew Allan are bearers of the Aaronic Priesthood who were called by an inspired bishop to team teach a family history class in their ward. These young men are representative of so many youth in their eagerness to learn and desire to serve.

Troy stated, "I used to come to church and just sit there, but now I realize that I need to go home and do something. We can all do family history."

Jaren reported that as he learned more about family history, he realized "that these were not just names but real people. I became more and more excited about taking the names to the temple."

And Andrew commented, "I have taken to family history with a love and vigor I did not know I could muster. As I prepared each week to teach, I was often nudged by the Holy Spirit to act and try some of the methods taught in the lesson. Before, family history was a scary thing. But aided by the Spirit I was able to step up to my calling and help many people in our ward."

These three young men experienced personally what all of us can feel as we grow in spiritual understanding by responding to invitations to act in doctrine. The most effective teachers are those who extend such invitations to learners whenever possible.

Personal Worthiness and "Getting Out of the Way"

You and I must learn to teach by the power of the Spirit. Of equal importance, however, is the responsibility to help individuals learn by faith and by the power of the Holy Ghost. In this regard, you and I are much like the long, thin strands of glass used to create fiber-optic cables through which light signals are transmitted over very long distances. Just as the glass in these cables must be pure to conduct the light efficiently and effectively, so we should become and remain worthy conduits through whom the Spirit of the Lord can operate.

In the eighteenth section of the Doctrine and Covenants, the Lord revealed to Joseph Smith, Oliver Cowdery, and David Whitmer the calling and mission of the Twelve Apostles in the latter days. The revelation includes this direct and powerful admonition: "You must walk uprightly before me and sin not" (v. 31). This inspired instruction applies equally to each one of us. Therefore, an essential prerequisite to becoming an effective gospel teacher is personal worthiness before the Savior and striving for the companionship of the Holy Ghost.

"And again, the elders, priests and teachers of this church shall teach the principles of my gospel, which are in the Bible and the Book of Mormon, in the which is the fulness of the gospel.

"And *they shall observe the covenants and church articles to do them,* and these shall be their teachings, as they shall be directed by the Spirit.

"And the Spirit shall be given unto you by the prayer of faith; and if ye receive not the Spirit ye shall not teach.

"And all this ye shall observe to do as I have commanded concerning your teaching" (Doctrine and Covenants 42:12–15; emphasis added).

We also must be careful to remember in our service that we are conduits and channels; we are not the light.

"For it is not ye that speak, but the Spirit of your Father which speaketh in you" (Matthew 10:20).

"Wherefore, I the Lord ask you this question—unto what were ye ordained?

"To *preach* my gospel by the Spirit, even the Comforter which was sent forth to *teach* the truth" (Doctrine and Covenants 50:13–14; emphasis added).

Note in these verses that we are ordained or set apart "to preach" the gospel. However, the Comforter is "sent forth to teach the truth." Thus, you and I are not the teachers; the third member of the Godhead, even the Holy Ghost, is the true and ultimate teacher.

This work is never about me and it is never about you. We need to do all in our power to fulfill our teaching responsibilities and simultaneously "get out of the way" so the Holy Ghost can perform His sacred work. In fact, anything you or I do as representatives of the Savior that knowingly and intentionally draws attention to self—in the messages we present, in the methods we use, or in our personal demeanor—is a form of priestcraft that inhibits the teaching effectiveness of the Holy Ghost.

"Doth he preach it by the Spirit of truth or some other way? And if it be by some other way it is not of God" (Doctrine and Covenants 50:17–18).

See DVD Segment 3

We should strive to apply in our teaching this timeless counsel from Paul:

"And I, brethren, when I came to you, came not with excellency of speech or of wisdom, declaring unto you the testimony of God.

"For I determined not to know any thing among you, save Jesus Christ, and him crucified.

"And I was with you in weakness, and in fear, and in much trembling.

"And my speech and my preaching was not with enticing words of man's wisdom, but in demonstration of the Spirit and of power:

"That your faith should not stand in the wisdom of men, but in the power of God" (1 Corinthians 2:1–5).

Effective gospel instructors know and understand that the Holy Ghost is the teacher, invite the constant companionship of the Holy Ghost into their lives through obedience and righteousness, do their best to "get out of the way," and avoid and overcome priestcraft as they teach and represent the Lord.

Teaching Is More Than Talking, Telling, and Lecturing

As the Savior sat on the Mount of Olives over against the temple with Peter, James, John, and Andrew, He declared:

"And the gospel must first be published among all nations.

"But when they shall lead you, and deliver you up, take no thought beforehand what ye shall speak, neither do ye premeditate: but whatsoever shall be given you in that hour, that speak ye: for it is not ye that speak, but the Holy Ghost" (Mark 13:10–11).

This same pattern for preaching was reiterated repeatedly by the Savior in the early days of this dispensation as He instructed missionaries to "open your mouths and they shall be filled" (Doctrine and Covenants 33:8, 10) and to "lift up your voices unto this people; speak the thoughts that I shall put into your hearts, and you shall not be confounded before men; for it shall be given you in the very hour, yea, in the very moment, what ye shall say" (Doctrine and Covenants 100:5–6).

Please notice in these scriptural instructions the important sequence of first acting in faith ("open your mouths"; "lift up your voices") before receiving a promised blessing ("they shall be filled"; "you shall not be confounded"). Interestingly, many of us routinely seek for precisely the opposite; we pray and ask for the blessing so we can act in faith (first fill our mouths so we can open them). But that is not the Lord's way or pattern. Faith precedes the miracle, and "ye receive no witness until after the trial of your faith" (Ether 12:6).

These scriptures emphasize a most demanding and exacting pattern for teaching and learning. Gospel instructors should recognize that they do not teach lessons; they teach people. They do not merely present lessons about gospel topics; they invite seekers of truth to experience the mighty change of heart. They understand that talking and telling alone are not teaching.

Teaching the gospel the Lord's way includes observing, listening, and discerning as prerequisites to talking. The sequence of these four interrelated processes is significant. Please note that active observing and listening precede discerning—and that observing, listening, and discerning come before speaking. Employing this pattern enables an instructor to identify and teach to the needs of learners.

As we observe, listen, and discern, we can be given "in the very hour that portion that shall be meted unto every man" (Doctrine and Covenants 84:85)—the truths to emphasize and the answers to give that will meet the specific needs of a particular individual or group. Only by observing, listening, and discerning can we be guided by the Spirit to say and do the things that will be most helpful to those whom we teach and serve. These essential components of teaching can and should be used before, during, and following a teaching episode. And an inspired teacher can apply these principles differently, appropriately, and effectively in a variety of teaching situations, such as conducting an interview, facilitating a

NOTES

discussion in a Sunday School class, discussing an issue in a family council, or speaking to a large congregation.

Mormon, the principal compiler of the Book of Mormon, is described as being "quick to observe" (Mormon 1:2). Recall that Ammaron counseled the youthful Mormon to both remember and record all of the things he had observed concerning his people (see Mormon 1:1–5). His ability to look, notice, respond, and obey provides an impressive example for us to study and follow.

Being quick to observe is a vital preparation to receive the spiritual gift of discernment. Discerning is seeing with spiritual eyes *and* feeling with the heart—seeing and feeling the falsehood of an idea, the goodness in another person, or the next principle that is needed to aid an investigator. Discerning is hearing with spiritual ears *and* feeling with the heart—hearing and feeling the unspoken concern in a comment or question, the truthfulness of a testimony or doctrine, or the assurance and peace that come by the power of the Holy Ghost.

See DVD Segment 9

I frequently have heard President Boyd K. Packer counsel members and priesthood leaders: "If all you know is what you see with your natural eyes and hear with your natural ears, then you will not know very much." His penetrating observation should help all of us to appropriately desire and seek for these spiritual gifts of observing, listening, and discerning.

Many of us have learned to teach without conscientiously observing, listening, or discerning. We simply talk and tell. Parents and gospel instructors who talk without observing, listening, and discerning teach neither lessons nor people. Rather, they talk to themselves in front of learners.

Treasure Up in Your Minds Continually

In the early days of this dispensation, the Lord counseled His missionaries to "treasure up in your minds continually the words of life, and it shall be given you in the very hour that portion that shall be meted unto every man" (Doctrine and Covenants 84:85). I invite you to consider the importance of the active admonition to "treasure up."

Treasuring up the words of eternal life is more than merely studying or memorizing, just as "feasting upon the word[s] of Christ" (2 Nephi 31:20; see also 2 Nephi 32:3) is more than simply sampling or snacking. *Treasuring up* suggests to me focusing and working, exploring and absorbing, pondering and praying, applying and learning, valuing and appreciating, and enjoying and relishing. (Do you have a favorite dessert or treat in which you take great delight? That is precisely what I mean by "relish.")

Recall how the sons of Mosiah—four truly remarkable missionaries named Ammon, Aaron, Omner, and Himni—"had waxed strong in the knowledge of the truth; for they were men of a sound understanding and they had searched the scriptures diligently, that they might know the word of God. But this is not all; they had given themselves to much prayer, and fasting; therefore they had the spirit of prophecy, and the spirit of revelation, and when they taught, they taught with power and authority of God" (Alma 17:2–3).

These valiant missionaries truly treasured up continually the words of eternal life.

And because the sons of Mosiah did not neglect or simply go through the motions of scripture study, because the doctrines and principles of the gospel were confirmed in their hearts as true by the power of the Holy Ghost, because this spiritual knowledge and understanding penetrated deep into their own souls, they became powerful gospel teachers. As Ammon described:

"Yea, I know that I am nothing; as to my strength I am weak; therefore I will not boast of myself, but I will boast of my God, for in his strength I can do all things; yea, behold, many mighty miracles we have wrought in this land, for which we will praise his name forever.

"Behold, how many thousands of our brethren has he loosed from the pains of hell; and they are brought to sing redeeming love, and this because of *the power of his word which is in us,* therefore have we not great reason to rejoice?" (Alma 26:12–13; emphasis added).

Ammon was a teacher who treasured up continually the words of eternal life and had the power of the word in him. And you and I need to follow the example of Ammon.

As representatives of the Savior, you and I have the ongoing responsibility to work diligently and to implant in our hearts and minds the fundamental doctrines and principles of the restored gospel, especially from the Book of Mormon. As we do so, the promised blessing is that the Holy Ghost will "bring all things to [our] remembrance" (John 14:26) and empower us as we teach and testify. But, the Spirit can only work with and through us if we give Him something with which to work. He cannot help us remember things we have not labored to learn.

"And now, as the preaching of the word had a great tendency to lead the people to do that which was just—yea, it had had more powerful effect upon the minds of the people than the sword, or anything else, which had happened unto them—therefore Alma thought it was expedient that they should try *the virtue of the word of God*" (Alma 31:5; emphasis added).

Gospel teachers need to treasure up continually the words of eternal life, rely upon the virtue of the word, and have the power of the word in them.

WE REPRESENT AND SERVE JESUS CHRIST

Effective gospel teachers know and understand whom they represent, why they serve, and what they are to do. In the sacred calling to teach, we are representatives and servants of the Lord Jesus Christ. We love the Lord. We serve Him. We follow Him. We are His agents.

As we teach, we do not represent our families, our friends, our academic discipline or training, or our professional experience. Rather, we represent Him. His purposes should be our purposes. His interests should be our interests. His work should be our work. His ways should be our ways. His will should become our will.

As representatives of the Redeemer, we teach the fundamental doctrines and principles of His restored gospel—the pearl of great price—simply and clearly both in our homes and at church. We do not present personal opinions or speculation. We do not dwell upon the unknowable mysteries in our personal study or in the things we teach. We proclaim and testify of restored truth in the Lord's way and by the power of His spirit.

We should remember Him in all that we think, in all that we do, and in all that we strive to become, and we should represent Him appropriately to all of Heavenly Father's children whom we serve—especially as we invite them to act in doctrine.

SUMMARY

For disciples of the Lord Jesus Christ, teaching is a fundamental aspect of serving. Teaching gospel truths by the power of the Spirit lifts souls, enlarges vision, strengthens commitment, and plays a vital role in both initiating and sustaining our turn away from self and to the Lord. As we both learn and teach the doctrines and principles of the restored gospel, we can be blessed to reduce the disparity between what we know and what we do.

"Thou therefore which teachest another, teachest thou not thyself?" (Romans 2:21).

Our responsibility as teachers extends far beyond talking, telling, and lecturing. Rather, the role of a gospel instructor is to invite learners to exercise moral agency in accordance with the teachings of the Savior. Only as learners act in faith can the power of the Holy Ghost penetrate into the heart of an earnest seeker of truth.

Effective service as a teacher requires personal worthiness, humility, continual treasuring up of the words of life, discernment, and an understanding of who we are as representatives of Jesus Christ. As we thus prepare ourselves for this sacred service, we become instruments in the hands of God to assist His children in finding answers to the questions of the soul—answers always contained in the fulness of the restored gospel of Jesus Christ.

Related Readings for Chapter Four

The two related readings for Chapter Four stress that teaching is a fundamental part of serving—in our families and in the Church. The fundamental role of a teacher is to invite learners to act in accordance with the teachings of the Lord Jesus Christ.

"More Diligent and Concerned at Home"
Ensign, November 2009, 17–20

As disciples of the Savior, we are not merely striving to know more. Rather, we need to consistently do more of what we know is right and become better. Both our words and our deeds are power-ful tools in the important work of teaching.

"The Hearts of the Children Shall Turn"
Ensign, November 2011, 24–27

We learn best by doing. The young women, young men, and children of the rising generation will be protected and blessed—in their youth and throughout their lives—as they "act in doctrine" and participate in family history and temple work.

CONSIDER

As I continue to turn to Christ, what can and should I do to more consistently and effectively turn outward in service?

CONSIDER

What am I learning about teaching and serving that can help me reduce the disparity between what I know and what I do?

CONSIDER

What can and should I do in my life to avoid and overcome priestcraft?

_____

_____

_____

_____

_____

_____

_____

_____

_____

_____

_____

_____

_____

_____

_____

_____

_____

_____

_____

_____

_____

_____

_____

CONSIDER

What can and should I do as a teacher to more effectively represent and serve the Savior?

My Own Questions to Consider

SCRIPTURES RELATED TO WHAT I AM LEARNING

Scriptures Related to What I Am Learning

AN INVITATION TO LEARN AND ACT		
What additional doctrines and principles, if understood, would help me to become a more effective teacher?	What can and should I do to "act in" those doctrines and principles?	How will I know if I am making progress in becoming a more effective teacher?

AN INVITATION TO LEARN AND ACT		
What additional doctrines and principles, if understood, would help me to become a more effective teacher?	What can and should I do to "act in" those doctrines and principles?	How will I know if I am making progress in becoming a more effective teacher?

AN INVITATION TO LEARN AND ACT		
What additional doctrines and principles, if understood, would help me to become a more effective teacher?	What can and should I do to "act in" those doctrines and principles?	How will I know if I am making progress in becoming a more effective teacher?

Sources Cited

Ballard, Melvin J. "The Sacramental Covenant." *Improvement Era,* October 1919.

Frankl, Viktor E. *Man's Search for Meaning.* 2006 ed.

Journal History of The Church of Jesus Christ of Latter-day Saints. Church History Library.

Lectures on Faith. 1985.

Lee, Harold B. *The Teachings of Harold B. Lee.* Edited by Clyde J. Williams. 1996.

Maxwell, Neal A. "O How Great the Plan of Our God." Address to Religious Educators, February 1995.

———. *We Will Prove Them Herewith.* 1982.

McConkie, Bruce R. *The Millennial Messiah.* 1982.

———. *A New Witness for the Articles of Faith.* 1985.

McConkie, Joseph Fielding. *Understanding the Power God Gives Us: What Agency Really Means.* 2004.

Monson, Thomas S. "Finding Joy in the Journey." *Ensign,* November 2008.

Oaks, Dallin H. "Taking upon Us the Name of Jesus Christ." *Ensign*, May 1985.

Packer, Boyd K. "The Cloven Tongues of Fire." *Ensign*, May 2000.

———. *Mine Errand from the Lord: Selections from the Sermons and Writings of Boyd K. Packer.* 1997.

———. *That All May Be Edified.* 1982.

Perry, L. Tom. "The Value of a Good Name." *Brigham Young University 1996–97 Speeches,* 1997.

Peterson, H. Burke. "Adversity and Prayer." *Ensign,* January 1974.

Romney, Marion G. In Conference Report, October 1963.

———. In Conference Report, October 1968.

Young, Brigham. In *Deseret News [Weekly],* July 28, 1869.

Young, Brigham. *Discourses of Brigham Young.* Selected by John A. Widtsoe. 1954.

INDEX